FIVE-MINUTE, FEEL-GOOD S
FROM THE PAST, HOPE FOR THE FUTURE,
AND JOY FOR TODAY.

SOUTHERN COMFORT

LYNN WALKER GENDUSA

Copyright © 2021 Lynn Walker Gendusa
Editing: Sally Apokedak; ALPS/Paraklesis Press
Interior Design: Sally Apokedak; ALPS/Paraklesis Press
Interior Illustrations: Michaele Flynn Prince
Cover photo courtesy of: Uwharrie Chair Company
Cover design: Aleksandar Petrović vajsman@gmail.com

ALPS
113 Winn Ct.
Waleska, GA 30183

Or email permissions.alps@ParaklesisPress.com for info or permissions.

Printed in the United States of America

First Edition 2021

ISBN: 978-1-947446-15-1

10 9 8 7 6 5 4 3 2 1

For David and the family we love.

Table of Contents

Author's Note

AFTER WRITING WEEKLY newspaper columns for over six years, I am humbled by the number of folks who suggested I compile them into a book. My first book of stories, *It's All WRITE with Me! Essays from my heart*, was released in 2018. *Southern Comfort* is a compilation of my essays written and published from 2018 forward, which generated the most responses.

America has endured much since 2018, and the world has changed. In the midst of COVID restrictions, it was often difficult to write stories about the family I couldn't see, friends who couldn't visit, and countless heartaches we couldn't heal. However, faith is what made me continue to reach out to readers to remind them that there was still hope in all things.

Messages about compassion, kindness, unity, and love are repeated countless times in my columns. I once said, "I read and talk about these words too much!" But I don't think we can ever overdo words of healing. We all can use peace in our lives, and the only way we can obtain it is through God and love.

The first story in this volume, "Her Name was Grandpa," is repeated from my first book. It explains who she was and how her name came to be. She is worth a repeat!

God bless you all, and I hope you enjoy finding some "Southern Comfort" in your lives.

Love,
Lynn Walker Gendusa
Roswell, Georgia
October, 2021

Family

My grandmother always said, "Put God first, family second, and all else will fall in the proper order." She was right about that.

Those who love us enough to teach us the ways of courage, compassion, and love by their example, light our paths to the future.

They forgive us when we fall, they applaud us when we rise, and we grieve when they are gone.

Our family is a bridge to the past, our comfort in the present, and our journey to forever.

Her Name Was Grandpa

HOW DO YOU love a child? How do you become the memory which evokes timeless smiles? Does your life exemplify your ethical beliefs and encourage children to follow you?

The greatest gift we have as adults are children in our lives. It doesn't matter if we are parents, grandparents, aunts, uncles, or friends of a child. Loving a little one and having the love returned is a more magnificent blessing than all the riches in the world. Period.

My brother, John, was three and watching his favorite Grandmother prepare biscuits. He watched as the flour hit the dough board and dusted the air. She was talking to him the entire time and laughed as the white powder settled on his eyelashes.

John was having a lot of trouble with her name, "Grandma." Since he was born with six grandmothers, he would easily get them confused. Two great, great grandmothers, two great grandmothers, and two grandmothers all residing in the same town! Plus, they all wanted to be called Grandma! Even though John had six grand-mothers, he had only one living grandfather.

Suddenly, while standing beside this grandma in her kitchen, he thought the solution would be to rename his favorite, making her special.

His coal brown eyes opened wide as he tugged his grandmother's apron, "You gonna be Grandpa!"

"John, I am Grandma, and he is Granddaddy," she replied as she pointed to her husband.

"You Grandpa, and he Granddaddy!" he emphatically stated again before stomping away.

From that moment on, nine grandchildren and eighteen great-grandchildren would forever call her Grandpa.

The name would also be representative of unconditional love. A love that allowed her name to be whatever these children wanted to call her.

Many people have crossed my path in life, but, without question, I have never known anyone quite like Grandpa.

She didn't just say, "I love you," she bestowed love in countless ways.

There was nothing she adored more than children. For those nine grandchildren who were in her life, we all knew that to be fact. When she played or talked with us, she became our age.

She even let us play with the wrinkles on her hand and make fun of her false teeth until she got new ones. She laughed at herself and was never embarrassed by any of us.

I can recall being in her small home with many of my cousins. Grandpa would play board games and tell us stories all day. Going fishing and enjoying picnics were Grandpa staples.

In the evenings, right before she went to her room to join my sleeping grandfather, she sat at the end of the hall and read her Bible. Her faith taught us the meaning of priorities.

When she played games, she never let any of us win. By honestly playing as hard as she could, she demonstrated for us how to have the grace to lose and how to be fair.

Her garden bloomed in July with white gladiolas that reached up to the sun. In her garden she taught us that out of dirt, toil, and care comes beauty.

When we stayed with Grandpa, she made sure she had everyone's favorite food in the house. She would cook until her old apron was soiled and dark. By her example, we learned how to show love.

It is hard for me to write all that she was and did in her ninety-seven years on earth. I could fill a book with stories about this remarkable, kind human being.

Grandpa's laughter fills my heart today. Her hands calm my soul, and her spirit still wraps me in unconditional love.

Over the years, I have written many stories about Grandpa. They have traveled across the country in publications large and small.

Her lessons, her love, and her beautiful soul still resonate and influence lives today. The name my brother gave her all those years ago is now a bold headline, and that is as it should be.

In loving memory of Nancy (Nannie) Melissa Pugh: 1897-1994

The Lesson of the Wiggly Worm

GRANDPA SAT ON the pond's bank with a fishing pole in her hand, an apron around her waist, a bonnet on her head, and a pail full of dirt and wiggly worms by her side.

"Grandpa!" I yelled. "Will you please put a worm on my hook?"

She did not answer, so I walked closer to her, thinking she might not have heard me.

As I held the old cane pole with the wormless hook waiting for her to put a creepy worm on it, she replied, "Honey, how old are you?"

"Grandpa, you know I am six!" I said, laughing.

"Well, you are old enough to put your own worm on that hook."

My eyes grew large, and my mouth opened in disbelief. My favorite grandmother in the whole world was not going to help me. I was dejected and certainly would not put that squirmy, ugly worm on the hook by myself!

I stomped my feet and shed a few tears, but Grandpa refused to notice me. She never uttered a sound except when she caught a big brim and yelled, "Whoopee!"

The fish kept biting, and I kept on pleading but to no avail. Finally, I knew I needed to dig in the bucket and find a worm if I was going to fish with Grandpa.

From then on, I became an expert in locating worms. My skills were well known to anyone interested in knowing them. Grandpa was about the only one who was.

We would fish nearly every day when I visited her, and she would even let me exaggerate about the size of the brim or bass I caught. Again, Grandpa was about the only one who pretended to believe me.

The funny thing about the lessons I learned sitting on the bank of a pond; they have stayed with me all my life. I realized that if you want to catch a fish, fulfill a dream, or live your best life, you must be brave enough to dig for it.

Life teaches us to keep trying and digging every day. There is not a day that goes by that does not require patience, work, and understanding. There is not a day when we cannot learn a lesson. Sometimes we are not open to knowledge, and often we lose patience. Some days we are not the best we can be because we were not motivated to be. Those are the days we let the big fish swim on by to be caught by someone else.

I recall very few days when Grandpa wasted a day. She did her chores, didn't complain, and rewarded herself by sitting in her folding chair by the pond when the day was done.

I also learned from fishing with my Grandpa how to teach a child to accept responsibility. Some grown-ups obviously missed that little tidbit of information. They blame everyone for not improving their lives, for their failed relationships, or for their inability to catch a big fish.

Grandpa was not an enabler of anyone who would not try, including a six-year-old. It started early with all of us. She was willing to listen to the crying, yelling, and begging because she wanted us to learn we were not going always to get our way, mainly when it was primarily the wrong way.

The lesson she taught me of not relying on others to do the hard work has served me well. Being a single parent of three children required me to be self-reliant and self-sufficient for much of my life. I never resented doing what was required to put a fish on the table to feed my children. Even if I didn't like the tasks—even if some of them felt like sticking slimy worms on hooks—I didn't mind them.

One of my readers once told me her favorite stories were about "Grandpa." I smiled as I thought about the many lives my grandmother touched. She still inspires by the salt-of-the-earth way she lived. Hers was a simple, rewarding life of cooking meals for her family, loving her husband, tending her garden, playing with children, laughing with her friends, adoring the Lord, and teaching a six-year-old a pailful of lessons by using a wiggly worm, a pole, and a hook.

Grandpa's Hope Chest of Treasures

IT DOES NOT seem that long ago when most of our homes included a piece of furniture, called a cedar, or hope chest. Originally constructed in the fifteenth century, they were dowry boxes—places to save and store items to be used in the first daughter's home after she married.

Many of ours in the south were used for storing blankets, sweaters, photo albums, and hidden secrets if you used the lock. Every one of my relatives and I owned this vital piece of furniture, including my grandmother, aka Grandpa.

Grandpa's cedar chest was covered in a golden mahogany veneer that matched her bed and dresser. Her bedrooms throughout her life were small, but she somehow expertly carved a space for this treasured piece. I would see her use the key to unlock the chest, throw something inside, and quickly lock it back. When I was young, I wasn't that curious about the contents because I usually tried to rush her to go fishing or play Rook.

One time when I was older, though, when Grandpa was in her late eighties and living in a small duplex in Tennessee, that old cedar chest of hers caught my attention. My mother and I had gone to visit her, and one afternoon Grandpa and Mama were in the bedroom talking, when I joined. Grandpa's old pocketbook was on the bed, looking worn and abused. When my mom saw it, she said, "Let's go shopping, Mama, and I will buy you a new purse!"

When I heard the word *shopping*, I quickly put on my shoes, but then Grandpa said, "Well, shoot Elizabeth, I think I have one in the chest!"

She retrieved the brass key from the drawer of her little dresser to unlock the chest. When she lifted the top, the mild scent of cedar wafted through the room. She rummaged through to the bottom and pulled an elegant navy-blue leather purse lifting it high above her head. "See, I knew I had me a new pocketbook in here!" she happily declared.

For a moment, Mom and I could not close our mouths as she held the beautiful purse with the original tags still attached. "Mama, where did you get that?"

"Oh, I am not sure, Elizabeth, but I think it was a Christmas present years ago from your brother. I was holding on to it like I do all these things in this chest."

Once she said that we both started to look in the secret space where Grandpa had collected a stash of finery fit for a queen. Gifts of robes, gowns, sweaters, perfumes, wallets, and shawls.

"Mama, why in the world have you not used these things?" Mom exclaimed.

My mouth was still open as I gazed at the contents of her secret world.

"Well, shoot, I was saving 'um!"

My mother replied, "Mama, how long are you planning on living? You know the purse will last years, and these are items you need and can use."

With that, my almost ninety-year-old Grandpa stated, "Well, I reckon you are right about that. I forgot that part!"

With that statement, my mouth finally started producing a laugh so loud that everyone joined in as Mama fell back on the bed in a howl.

We began to empty and organize the cedar chest contents with the hope that Grandpa would be able to have enough years to use all those gifts she had been saving for that ambiguous rainy day.

Why do we assume we are going to live forever? Why do we forget "that part" of living? I see people like Grandpa who put away the gifts of the beautiful things, to be used in an uncertain future. How many of us store our dreams in a hope chest in our minds?

We should take the plastic off the sofas and use the fine china on the table where crystal pieces hold the wine and the candles. I suggest we open our secret stashes of hopes and dreams and find a way to use them today. Who knows what we might discover when we unlock the hidden place where they reside?

When I leave this earth, I hope I've used up all my dreams, broken a few pieces of my fine china, and worn out my last purse.

Grandpa lived another ten years after we opened her secret box. In the end, the mahogany hope chest held nothing.

Grandpa's Quilt of Love and Laughter

IT IS ONE of those February gray days as I sit writing this piece, and this morning I felt slightly gray myself. I was a bit depressed for little reasons that I will not bore you with, but then the good Lord gave me a story, which immediately warmed my soul.

I am not surprised as remembering my grandmother usually brings joy. She could be humorous without trying and could be counted on to say or do something that would make me smile.

At the bottom of her cedar hope chest was an old, pieced quilt that was not quite finished–it still needed quilting. The top was hand-stitched with tiny pieces of folded men's clothing material. Old ties, shirts, and suits were cut into strips no wider than a half-inch, forming an utterly stunning log cabin design.

"Well, shoot, I reckon I should just throw this old thing away!" Grandpa declared as she held it up for Mom and me to view.

"Mama, did you make that beauty?" My mother questioned as my mouth refused to close to ask anything. The intricacy of this work of art left me speechless.

"No, I didn't stitch it; I bought it at a flea market a long time ago for fifty cents! I kept thinkin' I would quilt it 'cause I thought it was kinda pretty, but I never did. It sure was a waste of half-dollar, though."

When I was able to finally speak, "Grandpa, if you are going to throw it away, may I have it?"

"What do you want this old trashy thing for, honey?" She responded.

"It would make a lovely wall hanging, like a tapestry!" I answered.

Mother agreed, but Grandpa was still shaking her head as I carefully folded it and put it into a plastic bag.

A few years passed, and when I moved into a new home, I finally had a wall in my living room to hang Grandpa's trashy quilt. It was perfect, mixed with my antiques and family treasures.

After I was settled, the group came from Tennessee to Georgia to see the new house.

It was lovely to spend time with Grandpa, my mother, my mother's sister, Mary Ruth, and Aunt Helen. By the time we sat in the living room, my cheeks were already sore from the laughter. They were the best of the best, the cream of the crop, and I adored each one. When the Good Lord put me amid these delightful girls, it was a gift I never took for granted.

As we sat around the room, I noticed most of them were staring at the old log cabin quilt as it proudly dominated the room.

"Where did you find such a pretty quilt?" Mary Ruth asked.

Grandpa remained silent.

"What is that made from? It's so unusual!" Aunt Helen asked.

Grandpa remained silent.

Mama chimed in, "I saw in a magazine the other day, a quilt just like that one was going for over a hundred thousand dollars!" She then pulled out the magazine page she had saved to show the group.

Grandpa remained silent.

"Well, shoot!" Grandpa finally shouted. "I reckon I should have bought the other one! They were two for a dollar, but I didn't want to spend another fifty cents!"

While she was confessing to keeping the quilt in the bottom of the hope chest, getting ready to throw it in the trash, and could have purchased another priceless beauty for fifty cents, I was curled on the floor in laughter.

We teased her about that half-dollar until the day she died. I believe Mary Ruth and Helen were still miffed that they didn't have first dibs on the trashy quilt until they both passed away years later.

The antique quilt now hangs over the rail at the top of my upper stairwell. Folks walk through my door and spy it above them, but they do not see what beauty lies in between tiny stitches and old stories. Those memories are made just for me to hold in my heart, to chase cold gray days away, and to remember the priceless souls who still bring me blessings every day.

Is the quilt worth a hundred thousand dollars today?

No, it is worth far, far more.

Grandpa's Tennessee Christmas

ALL HOLIDAYS, ESPECIALLY Christmas, were joyous with Grandpa and Granddaddy. Grandpa wrapped presents with sticky bows and curling ribbons. They were never beautiful or fancy, but you knew there was something special hidden inside. Her tree was about the same. Colored lights hung with silver icicles and ornaments collected over the years. Nothing matched, and the more tinsel she could hang or throw, the happier she was. But underneath were many treasures.

Her house was also simple with its wood-burning stove heating the house and warming Granddaddy's hands as he came in from the lumber mill. He would stoke the fire as the aroma of cinnamon and cloves filled the air. And with her apron around her waist and flour scattered across a dough bored, Grandpa spent her holidays baking her scrumptious jam cakes as gifts for blessed souls.

But on Christmas day in 1965, the colored lights were still in their boxes, and no silver icicles hung from any tree. Grandpa had quietly made her jam cakes, that year, but Granddaddy was gone. He died suddenly in August, along with Grandpa's Christmas spirit.

We tried to console her, but she said, "Christmas won't ever be the same again, so I would just as soon be alone." It was the first time I ever knew my Grandpa to lose her infectious joy.

By the following Christmas, Grandpa was back in her warm kitchen, baking an abundance of jam cakes. Her love of Christmas was never quite the same, but her laughter and spirit were healing.

"Shoot, I was just feelin' sorry for myself! Christmas is about Jesus bein' born and the joy we feel because He was! I may not have a tree, but I got the Lord!"

A few years later, I made my Christmas buying list, but I couldn't think of a suitable gift for Grandpa. My typewriter was sitting near me, and I began writing a story about this remarkable, humble woman.

I was living in Georgia and decided to send the story to the Crossville, Tennessee newspaper. I never received a reply from the editor and began a new search for a meaningful present.

A few weeks later I received a phone call from Grandpa. "Lynn, what have you done?"

I immediately began to ponder all my misdeeds in life, and by the way she sounded, I figured God himself must have told her about them all.

After Granddaddy died, Grandpa moved the twenty miles from Monterey to Crossville, but she would travel back to her hometown every Wednesday to visit family. She always took the *Crossville Chronicle* for her sister to read. During this weekly road trip, she would stop and chat with her best friend, Hazel, in the Mayland community, halfway in between.

The old Dodge pulled into Hazel's driveway, and when she applied the squeaking brakes, a group of folks ran from the house screaming her name!

Scared to death, she hopped from the car, "What's happened! Is anyone sick?" She yelled.

"Nannie, did you not read that paper in your front seat?" Hazel asked as she pointed to the passenger seat.

"No, I didn't have time! Why? Whose obituary is in there?" She asked as she gazed at the surprised faces.

"Honey, bring your paper, and let's get in from the cold." Hazel insisted.

Once inside, Grandpa opened the paper to the second page as the crowd gathered around her.

MERRY CHRISTMAS, GRANDPA! was the nearly two-inch title running boldly across the top of the page. There were no ads, no other words other than those I wrote about the kindest woman I ever knew.

After her tearful thanks over the phone, she said as an afterthought, "Honey, did you know you can write?"

There are not many women who would allow their nine grandchildren and fifteen great-grandchildren to call them Grandpa. Few would bake delicate Christmas jam cakes as prized gifts or love others so much that an indelible mark would be left on their souls.

Today I write for publications, mainly newspapers, and it all began when love spilled on paper because my heart could not contain it all. Grandpa is now known beyond the Tennessee hills across the country through the stories I tell of this lovely, God-filled, thoughtful soul.

Merry Christmas, Grandpa! You were always Christmas to me.

Beneath the Pandemic Lies a Rose

IT WAS FEBRUARY in the Tennessee mountains when cold air seeped under windows while children buried themselves deep beneath quilts to find warmth. The trees were bare against a gray, winter sky as death loomed around every corner.

The year was 1920, and World War I was finally over but not the killing. The Spanish Flu traveled home with weary soldiers and targeted the most vulnerable. Within two years, five hundred million people worldwide were infected, and fifty million of those died. In the existing forty-eight United States alone, over six hundred and seventy-eight thousand succumbed to the illness.

And in one state—Tennessee—in the town of Monterey, people were dying, too. One woman, Rose Walker, rolled scatter rugs in front of her doors to stop the drafts and stoked the fire while she watched flames leap up the chimney. Her husband was deathly pale and shaking with fever when she heard her smallest child, Bertha Nell, cry out for her mother. Rose ran to her toddlers' bed to find her daughter hot to the touch as fear gripped her soul.

Before that February's end, both Rose's husband and daughter lay beneath the earth in the old cemetery in the hills of Tennessee.

My father was a small boy at the time his family endured this pain. He and three siblings survived, but until the day Dad left this earth, he cried each time he visited Bertha Nell's little-lamb-topped headstone in the old cemetery.

In the year 2020, a hundred years after Bertha Nell died, a pandemic once again invaded our lives. We were scared, and we had a right to be. There is no such thing as being too cautious or overprotective. Just as with the flu cases between 1918 and 1920, there were no drugs or vaccines to protect those who contracted the new disease. The H1N1 variant of 1918 was highly contagious as it drove small children, young adults, and folks over sixty five to graves across the world.

The COVID-19 of 2020 also was a new virulent with only experimental drugs or vaccines to combat the spread of its killing tentacles. What was different between the two pandemics was is the way information was spread through the media. We were better informed in 2020, and we were obligated to listen. We had the NIH, the CDC, the Public Health Service, and large companies joining our government to declare war on a vicious foreign enemy we could not see. We knew what we must do to keep it from killing fifty million people, but many would not follow the guidelines.

In times of trials, we must put aside our politics and blame. There will always be folks pointing fingers and stirring emotional pots, but what use is it to do so? Evil does not care about such trivialities. Its target is any life it can destroy. Every human being on earth needs to understand that when we are faced with global suffering, we all need to pick up our collective swords to fight and keep our eyes on the real enemy.

If you are a parent or grandparent, teach your children to love their neighbors. In 2020 my friend's son, John, and his family, lived close by.

"John, when are you all coming to visit this week and have dinner?" My friend asked her son.

"Mom, as much as all of us wish to see you as we usually do, I cannot expose you to a virus our family might unknowingly carry. It is too big of a risk. Even though we might want your help, you and Dad's health are more important than our desires."

With both John and his wife working from home with small kids in tow, they could have used the aid, but what was more important? A babysitter for their children or their mother's health?

When we think of others before our wants or inconveniences, we, like John, become bearers of unselfish love. And that, my friends, is how we survive when we face global challenges.

When we love our neighbors, we, like Rose, will survive the harsh sting of disease and the grief it causes—we will work again after storms of disaster upend us, we will restore our lives, and find the strength to do so. Rose continued to raise four children after death seeped into her home that February in 1920. She never remarried; she worked a myriad of jobs across Tennessee moving her growing brood with her.

She would face the Great Depression, another world war, and she would live on to tell us tales of survival and genuine, unselfish love. She would play old hymns on her pump organ and laugh with her friends and family. I was only ten when my grandmother's heart finally had given all it could.

I learned through those countless stories told by wonderful folks in ten short years to love with unselfish devotion.

I return to the mountains yearly, and as I pass by the little headstone in the old cemetery, a tear always falls to the earth below.

The Healing Power of Homemade Pie

COMIC STRIPS OFTEN entertain us with funny moments, but the cartoonist will occasionally introduce a bit of insight within their colorful panels. This was the case when Jan Eliot provided such wisdom in her strip called *Stone Soup*.

One of the characters is Alix, a nine-year-old, precocious girl, sitting at the kitchen table, watching her grandmother rolling the dough for a homemade pie.

Alix asked, "Gramma, why do you like to make pies so much?"

Her Gramma explained that when she was a young mother, they did not have much money, but she and her husband had an orchard abundant with pears, apples, and peaches. So, when they could afford only rice and beans for dinner, what lifted her family's spirits was a delicious homemade pie for dessert.

After hearing Gramma's explanation, Alix replied, "In other words ... before Prozac, there was pie."

Gramma ended the story with this statement, "That's what's

wrong with everyone! Not enough pie!"

Growing up, I recall my grandmother baking pies to deliver to folks. If you were ill or having a difficult time, or if you simply needed to chat with a friend, my grandmother had a pie for you. She regularly baked my brother his favorite chocolate pie and always made a cobbler for my mother when the blackberries were in season. I don't think I ever visited her that she didn't bake a pie out of love or compassion for someone.

I remember one summer day, her friend, Mrs. Harris, was ill. First thing on a Saturday morning, we visited Mrs. Harris's bearing an apple pie full of concern, healing, and affection. Before we left, Mrs. Harris was giggling with her friend and hugging me goodbye.

The tradition of pie giving was passed down from those ancestors who resided in the Tennessee hills to hearts who needed the pie's restorative power. Aunts, mothers, grandmothers, a few uncles, and even some grandpas inherited the gift of producing a mouthful of joy. My granddaddy couldn't make a pie, but he sure could cure a critter with his peanut brittle.

My mom could roll out the best crust on the planet. Plus, she had the artistic ability to create the perfect lattice top over her delicious fruit pies. She would serve them warm with a dollop of ice cream. Mom could dry tears and melt hearts with her delicious creations. I once dubbed her the *Queen of Pies*, and to this day, I believe she was.

Friends and family frequently question me, "Lynn, why do you insist on baking homemade desserts? You can go to the bakery and get a great pie or cake and not have to go through the trouble?"

My answer is always the same. "It's not the same!"

Generosity, kindness, and joy are only found in the work you go through to create them. Not everyone knows how to bake a pie, but they sure know how to gather flowers, write a sweet note, or hold a hand. When we use extra energy to lift another's spirit, we deliver healing. When we go to the trouble to love, we dish out trouble for hatred.

Our world is a busy place where texting emoji hearts, sad or smiling faces, makes it simple to share our emotions. We are *convenient* happy. Whatever makes our lives easier is the norm. However, our days will become more comfortable when our society becomes less hateful. And a peaceful world can exist only through loving each other enough to take time to be compassionate and understanding. Comforting each other is not about easy; it is about kindness, empathy, and giving. No emoji in the world provides the recipe for genuine affection.

"Before Prozac, there was pie," Alix declared.

I suffer from depression, and I understand needing medications for this illness. However, if my family and friends had been too busy to hug me, pray with me, or cook my kids' dinner through some of those wicked, dark hours, would I have made it? When those compassionate souls took the time to physically aid me, they helped me see a sunny day was on the horizon.

"That's what's wrong with everyone! Not enough pie!" Gramma happily told her grandchildren as she held her beautiful baked pie above her head.

What if we brought a homemade pie of kindness to the table of hate? What if we calmed anger with a dose of warmed goodness? What if we used more of our energy to create more empathy?

Then our grandchildren would learn, just like I did from my grandmother; when we take the time to create love, we might witness healing one pie at a time.

Gifts, Goodbyes, and Geysers

EVERY YEAR I spend countless hours preparing for my family's Christmas celebration. One year I had the house decorated and all the gifts wrapped by Thanksgiving. I was more prepared than ever before for my children to arrive and for the celebration to begin. I always overdo it, but that year was even more overdone than usual.

Folks often got upset with me because I did too much, but I always figured the bags under my eyes and the backaches were worth creating a memorable Christmas for all. About November each year, my best friend started to roll her eyes, and my husband threw his hands up in the air while waving the dreaded checkbook.

My stubbornness prevented me from looking at those eyes or the checkbook because I believed once they ate my cookies and enjoyed their new gifts, they would forgive and thank me. Nothing stopped my overcooking, my overspending, my over decorating, and my overdone Christmas stubbornness. That is until the Gendusa Geyser erupted in the front yard.

It was late on December 25 when we noticed a small pond around our mailbox. Water gurgled from the ground and spilled onto the street. We lived in a community with over seventy homes and an association to keep us from painting our house purple or putting a boat in our front yard.

The powers that be congregated around the forming lake on the 26th, and it was decided not to turn off the neighborhood's water supply because it was the holidays with visitors who prefer basic necessities.

"We should let the water flow into the street for a few more days. It probably won't get worse!" Declared the plumber and all those who just wanted to go home and enjoy Christmas leftovers and family.

On the afternoon of the 27th, my family prepared for another feast and more celebration when I noticed the pond was now an official lake. Muddy water no longer trickled, but currents were waving down the street, causing cars to swoosh through the flood.

Then as I watched the ocean rise, suddenly, as if we struck oil, muddy water shot sixty feet into the air and rained down onto our yard and street! Folks ran from their homes, taking videos and pictures. The Gendusa Geyser was headed for the history books.

The water was quickly shut off for the entire neighborhood, the plumbers returned, dug up the yard, repaired the old pipes, and put crime scene tape around the whole muddy mess, cautioning our neighbors that the Christmas Water Criminals lived there.

While watching the tidal waves, I learned a valuable lesson; I can prepare for Christmas or for any day, but who knows when a geyser will rain on our parade of preparedness. Maybe, just maybe, the mud taught me that even though we try to invent perfection and an ideal Christmas, in life, there is always something lurking to muddy the beautiful picture.

One night soon after, while my children were still there, we talked until the wee hours of the morning. Catching up with my children was always a treat and rare because my three lived in different parts of the country. The conversations caused tears and laughter, and as I sat on the floor, I noticed bits of wrapping paper and cookie crumbs on the rug. The disarray had formed its own path through my once idyllic Christmas-decorated home. Yes, perfection was gone, but was it?

Life's perfect moments are not found in the yard, or a house, or in the Hallmark version of a Christmas holiday. As I watched my three children laughing, supporting one another while creating a memory they would never forget, the heart of Christmas reigned in my imperfect home.

Finally, the children waved goodbye and headed to their faraway homes. They packed their gifts, once wrapped with beautiful bows, and they would soon forget what they received on that Christmas day. However, what they would recall would be the geyser in the front yard, the family of four musketeers still holding hands amid life's clutter, and the shared love that no amount of water could drown.

As I walked into a new year, I would make some changes or at least I would try to curtail my overzealous ways and enjoy this imperfect life the Lord gave me, including geysers, goodbyes, and all the gifts of my life.

Growing a Garden of Kindness

AFTER WRITING WEEKLY columns for years, and hearing people's responses, I have a few thoughts about our society. I have written stories that stretch from death to abundant life, depression to fried chicken, and every topic in between. However, when I write about my grandmother, or a pie that heals, or God's goodness, my computer lights up.

People are in a desperate search for human kindness. They crave goodness, fellowship, compassion, and understanding. In other words, they are all looking for hope that our world will turn away from judgmental attitudes and hypocrisy. They pray that bullying will somehow magically disappear, and that truth will always win.

Several weeks ago, my column, *The Healing Power of a Homemade Pie*, was inspired by the comic strip *Stone Soup* in the Sunday paper. Once the story was finished, I sent it to the cartoon's creator, Jan Eliot, who lives somewhere on the west coast. A short time later, I was surprised by her response.

"I read the column you wrote three times, and I so appreciate you taking my cartoon and honoring my work with yours." Jan began.

How lovely and sweet, I thought, but her kindness didn't end there. When the story gained a national audience, I heard from folks throughout the country.

From a comic strip to a column, to meeting authors, readers, and many others, I concluded, human kindness is like a seed planted deep in the earth. If you water it, take a bit of time to care, and clear the weeds, there is no telling how much beauty will rise from the soil and spread.

Every one of you has different opinions regarding every topic on which I could opine. Still, the one subject we can all agree on is that kindness is the key to living in harmony with one another. God calls us to be kind and lay down our swords of bias, mockery, and arrogance.

Many years ago, I was an Interior Designer based out of a large department store. A man was beginning his cross-country campaign to gain support for his first Presidential race. On a sunny southern day, he was scheduled to speak from our store's lower roof to a crowd gathered in the parking lot. I was aware of the event, but I had an important meeting with a client at about the same time.

I gathered my things for the meeting but required several wall-paper books, which were located near the store's other end—opposite from my office. As I walked to retrieve them, I was in such a rush, I overlooked several Secret Service agents until one grabbed my arm.

"Ma'am, you can't go any further because we have blocked this section off for safety." I pleaded with the gentleman. I desperately needed the books for the most relevant meeting of my young career.

"It won't take me, but I second, I promise. I will grab what I need and be out of your way before you know it!"

"Ok, but hurry!" He acquiesced.

My heart was racing as I grabbed the books, came out of the aisle running, and dropped them all when I abruptly stopped so as not to run into, or over, Ronald Reagan.

The books fell at his feet, and the Secret Service swarmed. After realizing I was not shot, I repeatedly said, sporting a bright red face, "Sir, I am so sorry, I was in such a dash!"

Governor Reagan laughed, leaned over, and began stacking the wallpaper books in my arms before the agents started helping. He assured me he was fine and joked about me slowing down.

Perhaps, positive power is found in compassion and not in winning a race. Goodness is always seen with a helping hand and not a fist. Kindness lives in those who take a moment to respond and not in those who never answer.

God is the caretaker who tends our gardens, but we are the ones who should always supply the water. If each of us helps Him, maybe our fields will be ripe with fruits of kindness, compassion, and love.

So, perhaps the search for kindness and curing many ills is in filling our water buckets.

"Live simply, love generously, care deeply, speak kindly, and leave the rest to God." ~President Ronald Reagan

The Hand of My Father

MY FATHER AND I had a quarrelsome relationship. It was rocky from the beginning, and I am not quite sure why. I was a sickly, willful child with a temper, who liked to dance and play basketball. Sometimes I would do both at the same time, which I thought was terrific.

Dad did not.

"Concentrate on what you are doing!" He would shout from the kitchen window near the basketball goal. That usually made me angry, so to spite him, I would quit both. I went through a stage when no matter how many times the rod was not spared on my backside, I couldn't stop making sassy remarks. He didn't understand my nature, and quite frankly, neither did I.

I spent the better part of my life trying to please my father, but I was not sure I ever did until recently. I was pretty confident he thought poorly of me when he left on a November day in 1999 to live among the angels. After his death, I would often reflect on our connection and talk to his spirit. Yet, I still felt strangely distant from this man I called Daddy.

Since I have been writing for the last few years, I ironically find myself becoming closer to my father. The stories he told me vividly return to my mind as if he spun them yesterday. The memories of his family, his friends, and his love for Mom are woven into sentences today. His emotional ways, sensitive nature, honesty, and humor still live through the words I write.

I am humbled when I study his ancestors' memoirs and recognize the blood that flows through me came from a mighty river of gutsy, hardworking, and groundbreaking folks. When I return to the place of my heritage, in the hills of Tennessee, I see him as I walk the streets where our family once strolled and as I pass the white clapboard house where I was born.

Before Memorial Day, 2019, I sat at my desk with a deadline approaching, knowing I needed to write a column regarding the holiday. I stared at my computer for a moment and asked God for help, and then my hands began to type a story that Dad recounted to me when I was a young girl. I did my research, edited, and finished the column. When I finished, I read it to my husband and afterward remarked, "I have no idea where that came from!"

Once it was polished, I sent it to my editors, and as a quick passing thought, also submitted the article to *The Tennessean* newspaper in Nashville. I again told my husband, "I just did the craziest thing!"

The story my father told me when I was a girl was printed as *The Tennessean*'s Memorial Day story.

When I was a small child, I recall my father sitting me in his lap every Sunday before church and reading the same Tennessee paper's comics.

Realizing that, I was assured Dad was still with me, and we finally understood each other's blessing. I appreciated this man more than I ever had. He taught me so many valuable life lessons I did not recognize until I started writing them down. The ups and downs along the rocky road had evolved into a smooth path of acceptance and peace. His love lives in stories that come to me in the middle of the night or as I stare at a blank computer. I know the hand of my father still guides me.

I read the comics every morning because Daddy always said, "they start your day with a smile." I find they do. He also abhorred laziness, and so do I. He loved people more than anyone I ever knew except maybe, me. Some things, like our fathers' lessons, never get old or fade away, or ever really die.

Father's Day is a special day for dads who are young, old, or in-between. It is also a special day of remembering the departed fathers who gave us the wisdom, the love, and the drive to carry on and heed their words.

I don't dance and play basketball at the same time anymore. Nor do I quit. I concentrate on getting the stories straight because I still enjoy pleasing my daddy. I finally learned.

In loving memory of my father, Ray Caraway Walker: 1914-1999.

When the Saints Go Marching In

AS A YOUNG Tennessee girl, I knew Louisiana was a southern state, but in my mind, New Orleans was a separate entity entirely. I heard the stories about the Crescent City citizens who celebrated with wild parades where beads were thrown, and folks acted strangely. Their floats looked nothing akin to my type of parades where homecoming queens and Santas waved to crowds. The tales regarding this city of jazz, crawfish, muggy weather, bayous, and crooked politicians played in my mind like a mysterious backdrop for a novel.

It is funny how I recall my original thoughts of New Orleans as if it were a portent of what was to come. Little did I know that forty-eight years later, my last name would change to Gendusa.

A group of immigrants from Sicily landed in New Orleans at the turn of the 20th century and began pursuing the American dream. They were bakers by trade and opened a shop which sent the smell of fresh bread wafting down the old streets wooing Italian, French, Irish, and Cajun customers. The Gendusa Bakery became known for producing the Po' Boy bread used for the famous sand-wiches initially created during the Great Depression.

Yes, I married the most Italian (with a bit of French thrown in) Crescent City-born guy I could find. A few months after our rela-tionship began, I met David's mother when we went to New Orleans for his high school class reunion.

My first impression of Doris Gendusa was how adorable she was. Perfectly coiffed bleached hair, long dangling earrings, polished pink nails on fingers where diamonds sparkled just like her eyes. When she walked, she danced, and when she talked, I finally deter-mined that the GOLF of Mexico meant Gulf. She was joyful, funny, and could create delectable dishes that I would never forget.

David was a former student at a private Catholic high school for boys. At the reunion, Doris sat with us because parents are invited to class reunions. What?! Folks were reserved and proper as we sat for dinner and listened to the music of a classmate famously known for playing classical Chopin like Chopin.

I began to doubt we would listen to Chubby Checker and dance the Twist as my classmates and I did at our reunions. Were we in New Orleans, or had we taken a cultural detour?

After we dropped off the delightful Doris, we joined a group of David's friends and their wives at a local honky-tonk down the street from the school. By the end of the evening, trust me, I knew we were in the heart of New Orleans.

My first parade in the Mardi Gras city was the Irish-Italian Pa-rade held every year in March. Floats were filled with the Irish throw-ing beads and the ingredients for Irish stew. I was shocked as I heard myself pleading for cabbage and potatoes as my arms were flung in the air!

When the Italian men in black suits and red ties walked toward every girl in Jefferson Parrish who lined the parade route to give them a rose and a kiss, Doris roared with laughter at the fool I made of myself.

When David was five, Doris told me he sat down to watch the Macy's Thanksgiving Day parade on television. A short time later, he told his mother he was going outside to play.

"Honey, don't you like watching the parade with all the floats?" She asked.

David answered, "Mama, that parade is no good. Those people on floats don't throw anything!"

After fourteen years, I have learned more than a textbook could teach about the mysterious, spirited New Orleans and its diverse citizens. I understand they live for food because they thrive on companionship. They have parades because they love experiencing joy and celebration, and these things bring folks together on their streets. Their history runs deep, and they keep their various heritages and customs close to their hearts. New Orleans residents band together as one to defend their plot of American soil and they trust their strength to survive any wrath Mother Nature decides to deliver.

Doris passed away on a cool January day in 2020. The New Orleans daughter, whose bright smile, and dimpled cheeks, showed a daughter-in-law the ways of a culture few understand.

As we departed her Celebration of Life Service, two family friends who, earlier in the service sang a hymn and played the guitar, suddenly began performing, *When the Saints Go Marching In*. When the Big Easy natives hear that song, they immediately form a line and wave handkerchiefs.

I swear I saw Doris at the end of the line waving goodbye to her mysterious, wondrous Crescent City and the people she cherished.

In loving memory of Doris Mae Gendusa: 1928-2020

Sorry, Rook, Scrabble, and the Bible

THERE ARE MANY shortcomings I possess, which I admit are my fault. I talk too much, I don't clean under the sofa often, and I don't turn off lights as I should. There are many more flaws, but the editors only give me so much room in the newspaper.

However, two of my shortcomings are not my fault; I inherited them from my ancestors. If my family's DNA were tediously sifted through, scientists would find a lineage of stubbornness and competitiveness stronger than any physical trait yet seen in laboratory testing.

My great-grandmother, Mollie Sparks, was known to be the most willful woman born in the hills of Tennessee. She could put her foot down like no one else. If an earthquake shook the world, her size-four shoe was not moving off the ground.

My father and I would snicker when my mother would declare, "Grandmother Sparks was the most stubborn woman I ever knew!"

We laughed because mama was exactly like her grandmother,

except she wore a size-eight shoe. Mama also exhibited an added dose of competitiveness, inherited from Mollie's daughter, my grandmother, whom we called Grandpa.

There are many competitive, gifted, famous folks in the academic and sports worlds. International Academic Members and Hall of Famers would squirm in their competing seats if they faced the lady known as Grandpa.

She was a skilled Scrabble player, but she either threw away the rules or lost them at some point in time. We all learned to play Scrabble by Grandpa's rules. It never occurred to any of us that there was another way to play. And, Lord knows, if we had known there was another way to play, we would not have told Miss Also Stubborn Grandpa about it. She might have thrown her size-seven shoe at us!

Once, when I was on a trip with three friends, we found a Scrabble board in the house we rented, and we decided to sit down for a friendly game.

After a few minutes, Michele asked, "What kind of Scrabble are you playing, Lynn? This is sure different from how I learned to play!"

"Well, the only way to play Scrabble is to use Grandpa's rules!" I responded.

I am not sure how I convinced three others to play the same way, but I did. I think you see the stubborn gene didn't fall far from the heritage tree, right?

Whether we played Scrabble, Rook, or Sorry with Grandpa, she played with a fierceness that would make Tiger Woods weary. She could out fish anyone, outsmart most of us, and she would never forfeit a game to a beloved five-year-old just to be nice. No, she was going to teach us that those who win, win fair and square.

We all inherited her competitive nature, and we all loved a good challenge. Mama became a champion golfer after playing for only three years. She also could trump anyone in a Bridge game (though, she was not likely to beat Grandpa at Rook). I couldn't match either one's abilities, but I did learn a far more valuable lesson by observing these priceless women.

Watching their skill and determination, as well as their stubborn and competitive natures, convinced me I could achieve almost anything if I put my size-six shoe down.

All who know me know I am stubborn and competitive. I once apologized for these characteristics, but now, I simply say, "It's not my fault!"

And truth be told, I am not really sorry. I am filled with gratitude for these exceptional women who believed they could accomplish anything if they worked hard enough. They never once assumed they couldn't win a game, couldn't handle a problem, or couldn't achieve a goal.

Every night, after Grandpa had caught all the fish for the day, hoed in her garden, cooked three square meals for the family, and beat us all in a final game of Sorry, she sat alone to read her Bible before going to bed.

"Grandpa, how many times have you read the entire Good Book?" I asked her one time.

"Well, shoot, I reckon, dozens." She declared without any fanfare.

"What have you learned?" I questioned.

"Well, I reckon I learned how to live. I learned I could handle any ol' problem, achieve almost anything I set my mind to, and I would win if I only believed. My mama taught me the Bible held all the answers, so I just keep on looking for 'em."

Sometimes the answers to the questions on how to play the game of life are not so far away. They are given to us by those who walked in extraordinary shoes before us, and the Good Book still shows us how to play by the rules.

Between the Outhouse and the Cherry Tree

HER HOME ONCE sat three concrete steps up from street level on a large plot in the small town of Monterey, Tennessee. It looked as if it belonged in the country instead of near downtown. The old house with its weathered brown boards and sagging front porch would appear to some as an eyesore, even in a tiny town.

The front porch held an assortment of worn wooden chairs where she and her daughters sat to shell beans, shuck corn, and escape the summer heat swelling inside. They watched as folks passed by and exchanged a wave or shouted a "howdy-do." Once the neighbors saw those smiling faces, the house wasn't in as bad shape as they initially thought.

Funny how our eyes are fooled by acts of kindness.

Inside the tidy house was a parlor that opened to a large kitchen equipped with a wood-burning stove, stacks of iron skillets, and a cabinet that held everything from baking soda to castor oil. On the large table, anchored in the room's center, sat a wooden dough bowl where fresh biscuits were kneaded every morning, and folks enjoyed hot coffee poured from an old, dented, enamel pot.

Outside the kitchen door was a small rear porch near the well that supplied fresh water. Hoes, rakes, and buckets surrounded a small wobbly chair that could hold a weary soul after a long day. In its summer splendor, the garden rested on the back edge of the property just beyond the cherry tree and the outhouse with its half-moon carved door.

In the summer, I loved to play between the outhouse and the cherry tree behind my great grandmother's house. The old tree teemed with ripe, red, tempting fruit. I would climb to pick as many cherries as possible before I got caught by the mighty hands of my tiny, fierce great grandmother, Mollie Sparks.

"How many times have I told you, young'un, to not eat too many cherries because you gonna' spend the rest of your day in that outhouse!" she would yell.

I knew I was immune to the side effects of too many cherries, and when she turned to walk back into the house, I continued climbing the tree to retrieve more delicious red goodies.

One day, however, I got sick, and she swore it was those cherries. I knew it was just a bug because, on that day, I had not climbed the tree. But the castor oil came out of the cabinet, and even though my mother was present, she knew she could not stand up against her grandmother's will. I took the dreaded castor oil, and to my surprise, it wasn't as bad as I feared it would be. Plus, it sure made the bug fly away.

The funny thing about facing fear: once you do, it usually flies away.

When my great Uncle Casto moved into the old house with his mother, Mollie, in their later years, he and the rest of the family, insisted she install indoor plumbing.

"What do I need plumbing for?" she asked her son and son-in-law. "I have been doin' just fine all these years. That's just a waste of a dollar!"

They built an indoor bathroom anyway, and of course, she stubbornly refused to use the new facilities until one night it became so icy in the mountains, she gave in. Afterward, she gathered the boys, and humbly said, "I know I sometimes can be right willful, but I do thank you."

The funny thing about misplaced stubbornness: humility will usually stop it.

Well into her eighties, Great Grandmother Sparks got into an argument with Casto over who grew the best garden. So, they built two to see which one would reap the best produce. Casto noticed his mother's hoed rows were crooked, but he also knew cataracts blurred her vision. Many nights, when his mother was fast asleep, he took his hoe and, with a flashlight in hand, straightened her rows and cleared the weeds she missed.

Both gardens bloomed beautifully that summer with Grandmother Sparks laughing with glee, "See, mine is the best! I won because I have fewer weeds!" She never knew just why her garden was ripe with beauty.

The funny thing about unselfish love: it does make our spiritual gardens grow.

I went by the old property the last time I visited the Tennessee town where I was born. Mollie's home is long gone, and now there are brick steps that lead up to a fine brick house with no front porch. It is pleasing to the eye but not as beautiful as the old run-down house, once filled with smiling faces and joyful giving hearts.

The funny thing about my life: I learned an awful lot from those fantastic folks who once walked between the outhouse and the cherry tree.

Happy Trails to You

DAD HELD MY hand as we strolled toward the mammoth beast he wanted me to ride. Since I was only five, the horse resembled a giant dragon but didn't appear as if he could spew fire. Dad hoisted me into the saddle as I realized horses are sure larger in real life than they are on television. I tried not to be frightened, but my heart pounded.

The horse must not have taken too kindly to the kid on his back and before we took one hoof-sized step, he bucked. The next thing I knew was I was lying in the dirt gasping for air. Yep, either the fall knocked the breath out of me, or I decided to quit breathing so I wouldn't have to ride that dragon!

Luckily, the only thing that was hurt was my dream of riding horses like Roy Rogers and Dale Evans did on TV. I even had a cowgirl outfit and boots to play the role of their kid one day! But as I lay in the dirt, my illusions were shattered. I concluded that there was no way anyone would put me back in a saddle again.

Well, that was what I believed before Dad picked me up off the ground and put me back on the dragon as I screamed and kicked. However, this time the horse didn't buck. A handler led the horse and me around the oval track while I began to hum *Happy Trails to You*. Shoot, maybe I would be on the television with Roy and Dale by Saturday if I kept riding so well!

There were many times during my life when my dreams landed in the dirt. Times when I felt nothing would make me believe I could put my shattered hopes back together. Many of us have attempted to conquer fears, tame a beast, try and try, only to fail repeatedly. When Dad made me ride again so soon after I fell, he taught me that no matter what, if an attempt doesn't kill you, you need to keep trying to find your *happy trail*.

My father often needed to push me. From riding a bike to learning to drive a car to believing that I could do anything if I put my fear aside long enough to try. Many times, I kicked and screamed through my panic. I shook my head, "no," and I stomped my feet, but ultimately, I succumbed to his determination.

When the world began traveling by automobile, my grandmother decided car-driving was not for her. She wanted someone else to drive her, or she would just walk to get what she needed. She put her stubborn foot down and was unruffled by her husband's attempts to plop her in the driver's seat.

Granddaddy knew her reluctance was based on fear, and he finally coaxed her to get behind the wheel.

"Ok, but I am not learning to drive on the road!" Grandpa declared.

"Well, Nannie, where are you going to learn if not on the road?" he responded.

"In the front yard!" she announced, putting that stubborn foot smack down on the hardwood floor.

Granddaddy looked out the window noticing the yard was full of trees. How was he going to keep her from running square into one?

Grandpa sat in the driver's seat with granddaddy by her side. They both feared for their lives as they started the engine. She dodged trees, slammed on brakes, and swerved so hard she almost threw her husband out the passenger door. Yet, somehow in the tree-studded front yard, she miraculously conquered the beast.

When Grandpa was around ninety-five, her children finally took her little red Dodge away because of her worsening dementia. When I visited her one day, I asked, "Grandpa, how are you feeling?"

"Shoot, I'd be fine if they would give me my Dodge Dart back!" She said as she stomped her foot on the tile floor.

Sometimes when we conquer our fears to fulfill our dreams, we find complete joy like my grandmother did once she started putting the car on the road. I assure you she never drove over thirty miles per hour, but that didn't matter to her one bit.

There is not one day too late to put your worries aside and work a dream into reality. Find the *happy trail* for you and remember to get back in the saddle if you fall.

"Happy trails to you, 'till we meet again." ~Dale Evans

Where the Hilltops Kiss the Sky

"Home is where one starts from." ~T. S. Eliot

I STOOD IN front of the white clapboard house, which lay in stark contrast to the bright green surrounding it. Rolling hills of lush spring grass cascaded down the backyard that was alive with budding hardwood trees and birds flitting between the branches. The simple structure needed a bit of work, but what a sight to behold. My parents built the house a few years after they married in 1939.

While viewing the home from Hoyt Street, I thought I heard the faint sounds of a baby crying. But it was just a memory planted deep within my soul.

Mama gave birth to her three babies in this pretty house in Monterey, Tennessee. The first one, Betty Ray, lived only three days, and when she passed, Daddy cried beside Mama's bed where she lay. Betty was buried a mile away in the old cemetery. The house grew quiet that cold February day as grief passed through the halls and down the rolling hills.

After a while, the sound of a healthy boy's chatter filled the still summer air. Delight returned to those who played in the yard, sledded down the hills in winter, and laughed at the antics little John pulled. "That boy is a handful, to say the least!" My parents would tell each other.

Six years later, when the leaves turned amber in the autumn, I was born in the same bedroom—down the hall in the pretty white house on Hoyt.

I thought of my mother and her life as I viewed my old home, watching the front door, expecting it to open. Expecting to see her standing there, calling us in for supper. However, Mama, Daddy, and John were with Betty Ray by then. But I had my memories of all that began there in the little white house and all the lives touched by those who once called the place home.

My mother and father grew up in that town where everyone knew everyone else, and most of them were related. And even though we moved away when I was young, we often returned to see old friends and kinfolk.

Mother always loved visiting her best friend, Violet, during those trips back home. They grew up together, playing sports, sharing secrets, and remained close throughout their lives. Violet is gone now. She passed away at the age of 102 in 2020. She rests up the hill from Mama in the old cemetery a mile away.

I left the old home to drive around the town. As I passed the place where the old high school once stood, I believed I heard a basketball dribbling on the newly waxed gym floor. Crowds were cheering as Mama and her best friend continued making point after point to win their championship game.

I expected them to burst through the gym doors dressed in their purple and gold with a trophy held high, but the door remained closed, and I realized it was just their legacy planted deep within in my soul.

The lake at the edge of town surrounded by a vast farm was probably the most beautiful place on earth. I was always told that, so I knew it was true. As I watched the wind move the water to lap onto the shore, I saw my brother swimming in the shallow end as Daddy tried to catch another big bass. Mama was unloading a picnic basket of sandwiches and cookies on a grassy knoll near the lake's edge. Folks happily waved as they passed by in canoes and skiffs.

The wind calmed, and all went silent because I knew it is just a beautiful scene painted deep within my soul.

I drove to the old lumber mill, but it was no longer there. Yet, I heard the mill whistle blow, telling all their workday was done. I saw my father, excited to go home where Mom had fried chicken waiting. Since that was Dad's favorite, he was in a hurry. I smiled at the memory. It was the simple things that made my father so happy: a family, a pretty little house, a good job, and fried chicken.

I looked up to find the whistle. It was gone, but the sounds of it all were frozen in that place that was planted deep in my soul.

People say you can't go back home, but I disagree. Memories carry us to a place where we clearly see those we adored—those we long to see again. Those people who taught us the importance of family, roots, connections, and love prompt us to return to relish their memory planted deep within our souls.

The motto for Monterey, Tennessee, is, "Where the hilltops kiss the sky." I swear I felt Mother kiss my cheek that day when I went back home where I began.

In loving memory of my mother, Elizabeth Pugh Walker: 1919-2010

Friendship

We do not always agree with our friends, but we can all agree that friendship is a gift from God. Perfect in its imperfection and necessary for a healthy soul.

Without friendships, the world would hear less laughter, see less hope, and rivers would overflow with tears.

A needed hug from a friend is like a warm blanket surrounding you on a cold, gray day.

Friends are more valuable than gold. Those we meet are meant to be.

Treasure them all.

A Parade of Human Kindness

2020 BROUGHT FORTH not only a killing pandemic. It also shined a light on the best and worst in all of us. We experienced it all, from the discord found in the political environment to the medical community's united front. The good, the bad, the love, and the hate, resided side by side. Neighbors, friends, and family members fought over politics and who was right and who was wrong until there was talk of another civil war.

There was so much bitterness, but I witnessed something one weekend that renewed my faith in the best of humankind. Sometimes life unfolds to reveal a bit of healing and a glimmer of hope that appears divine.

Some people seem to love strife. Some enjoy controversy—they spread distrust to gain fame and fortune. Others put their fellow citizens in harm's way to make a point or prove a theory or because they want power. Humans can become evil, malicious, and selfish, but that is not what I saw on the 2nd day of January 2021.

My friend turned a page on age that day. Several years ago, when I turned her age, she, and a few other close friends, hosted a luncheon for me with family and friends. Folks hugged, shared a meal, and laughter roared as they told old stories. My friends went overboard, but I will always remember that wonderful day.

I never thought I would not be able to do the same for my pal on her birthday over three years later. Two other friends and I tried to come up with safe ideas to celebrate this beloved woman.

January 2 is not the best day for a birthday anyway, even when there is no pandemic. No one gets their picture in the paper for being the first baby born on the day after New Year's Day. Many times, one's birthday presents combine with the Christmas gifts. Plus, folks are so tired by January 2nd, they most certainly do not enjoy the idea of throwing a party.

How could we safely celebrate, without a festive, large gathering, a good friend who was born on the day after fireworks lit the sky? Of all the people I have known in my life, she is the one who seems to know everyone. I laugh at the number of friends she has. I could not keep up with them all if I tried, nor could I write that many Christmas cards. There is just something about her genuineness and kindness that draws people to her like a magnet. She is far nicer than I am, but she hangs with me anyway, puts up with my rants, and forgives my many foibles.

I had seen those car parades where people safely celebrated a birthday or a significant event during the pandemic, so we thought that might be a good idea. I am not sure how many people I emailed, telling them to spread the word that on January 2, 2020, there would be a surprise parade for Deborah.

We did have the little luncheon with just the four of us, but we used a ruse to coax her outside, in front of my house, precisely at noon. Around the curve, my husband drove the lead in his bright red car topped with balloons, and when Deborah saw it, she looked puzzled. As far as one could see, car after car rounded the curve. Many, adorned with more balloons and signs, held several passengers while countless horns blew as they inched closer.

"What have you done?" Deborah shouted as she ran into the street. People presented her with cards, gifts, champagne, and air hugs as each one greeted their surprised friend.

I watched as the smiling people seemed to relish where they were, who they were celebrating, and the complete and utter joy of being a part of creating happiness for a person they loved.

Those who participated had differing beliefs, attitudes, and personalities, yet their diversity did not break their mutual bond of friendship.

Perhaps, we can avoid civil wars if we remember we find happiness when we unite to create joy for one another.

January 2 became a day not many will forget, including the girl who said, "It was the best birthday ever!" As for me, I was able to watch the light of human kindness shine on the best parade of my life.

Walk a Mile in His Shoes

I WAS DELIGHTFULLY honored to be asked to speak at a civic club meeting. After my response, "Of course!" I began to ponder the topic.

I conferred with trusted friends and decided it would be "Life Lessons." As I was settling on a subject, an old photograph of my mother fell out of an album I was dusting.

Her dark brown eyes seemed to be searching my face as I studied hers.

Elizabeth Walker was stunning and dignified with a quiet disposition. She spoke softly, always choosing her words carefully. I never heard her yell or demean another human being.

Between Mom and her mother, I learned many life lessons, but the first rule they both lived by, was, "Always walk a mile in another's shoes before believing you know the answer."

In the third grade, a little boy sat in the back of our classroom. He was always dirty, his clothes ragged, and often, his odor permeated the room. Kids mocked him, shunned him, and I, too, found it difficult to tolerate the stench. However, before I could join with the others in taunting the boy, I recalled hearing my mother's words, "Walk a mile in his shoes."

His shoes were dusty brown leather with laces that did not match, and socks turned gray with age. His blond hair curled around his smudged, somber face. When I put on his shoes, in my eight-year-old mind, my heart hurt, and as I held my nose, I decided to be a friend to the boy who had no friends.

"Mama, I have to pinch my nose, but I'm trying to walk in his stinky old shoes!" I proudly declared.

A wry smile accompanied her response, "Well, that's good because God will not need to hold his nose when He is around you."

At the time, I never understood why The Almighty might have to hold his nose when I took a bath every day, but as the years passed, it became abundantly clear. Stench and dirt born within our souls is worse than the foul odor of unwashed bodies.

Compassion is the number one lesson we all must learn before we acquire understanding. We may have never experienced hunger, but if we put ourselves in the shoes of those waiting in line for food, we begin to feel the pain of starvation.

Unless we have endured discrimination, been bullied or mocked; lived in poverty, wracked with pain, hopelessness, or loss; do we really comprehend how any of it feels?

No, we do not.

God will begin to hold his nose because of our filth if we do not put on the clean clothes of understanding and empathy.

The most intelligent and satisfied people I have met were those who were educated in insight and love. They never owned the shiniest cars or the biggest houses, but they had no need for them. These were people who understood the art of living—brilliant folks who knew this earthly life is made richer by humility, sharing, kindness, and easing others' burdens.

My grandmother, aka Grandpa, gave away more things than I believe she ever kept. Whether it was her canned green beans, pies, or quilts, they found their way to those who wanted or needed them more than she did. She over cooked, over cared, over loved, and over enjoyed her life.

"Grandpa, what are you going to do with all those white gladiolas in the garden?" Every summer, the same flowers climbed toward heaven, row after row.

"Honey, they go to the church on Sunday and then to the nursing home after that. Everybody always needs a flower!"

Everyone should have a heart like Grandpa's. Her life was abundantly full because she gave it away one flower, one pie, at a time, in doses of kindness all the days of her life. She continually walked a mile in other people's shoes and felt every pebble under each sole.

I also found a photograph of my third-grade class in the old album. Not everyone is in this snapshot, but I am in the first row with Sally, Mary Margaret, and Wanda. I recognize most of them, along with the boy in the back with his sweet face smiling at the camera. His pale eyes search mine as I look back to the year when we were eight.

It was the year I walked a mile in his shoes and was blessed by the lasting lesson it taught me.

The Western Flyer and the Newspaper

YEARS AGO, WHILE standing near a freshman class window at a Tennessee high school, I noticed a large snowflake fall from the sky. By the time the class bell rang, the snow was starting to settle on the yellow buses lining up near the front door to carry us home. We needed to leave in a hurry because every white delicate falling flake stuck to the pavement like glue.

Quickly the town of McMinnville, Tennessee, was covered with a blanket of snow. Kids ran home to be wrapped in layers of clothing—shortly after, they emerged adorned with earmuffs, mittens, and rubber galoshes. Many of us lived near Dr. Smoot's house, which sat atop a perfect sled-riding hill. The gracious doctor and his wife allowed their property to become public transportation for sleds and anything else deemed suitable to glide swiftly down their hill.

Nearly a foot of snow settled on the downtown streets, and schools were closed for days. The Smoot's land was packed with sled riders and squealing kids who were often invited indoors for Snow

Cream, cookies, and a bit of warmth.

I didn't own a sled, but Barbara and her sister, Jane, did, until the day it broke beyond repair as one of us raced it down the slope.

"Barbara, what are we going to do without your sled?" I screeched.

We collected piggy bank money and a bit more cash from our parents and headed to the Western Auto store downtown on foot.

The Barren Fork River runs through McMinnville, and for us to reach the store, we needed to cross the large steel Westwood Bridge. When one needs a sled to slide down Smoot Hill, one has no fear of raging water, out-of-control cars, or freezing feet.

Once we arrived at the hardware store, the smell of hot cocoa mixed with pipe tobacco warmed our senses. Sitting on a top shelf was a shiny, new Western Flyer sled needing a new home. We quickly paid, drank complimentary cocoa, and headed back to the bridge.

We took turns pulling one another on the sled as we started across the narrow walkway attached to the side of the bridge. We laughed with delight as we tried to run in the deep snow. Smoot Hill was waiting, for heaven's sake!

We were so taken with our Western Flyer we failed to notice a truck stopped to see what we were doing. Two local newspaper reporters with a camera stepped out. They wanted to take our picture and find out why three girls would trek three miles to town, over an icy river, and defy frostbite.

"To get a new Western Flyer sled!" we yelled in unison. And, just like that, we were on the front page of the local paper.

Thinking about this so many years later makes me think about what we've lost with the closing of many brick and mortar stores and with the advent of digital everything. It is my duty as an old fuddy-duddy to curtail the madness.

Today we all love the convenience of online shopping, apps for reading digital news, and less time spent searching for items. Yours truly has found the internet an absolute delight when connecting with old friends and needing pertinent information of any kind.

Having said all that, what do we miss when we *save time* shopping or reading an actual newspaper? Let's go back to the beginning of the story. While we are staring at our iPads, phones, and computers, did we miss the snowflake that just fell to the ground below?

And as good as Amazon Prime is, there is no way we could have received the sled faster than it took three girls to acquire the red metal and wood flyer at the Western Auto store. Plus, Amazon does not supply complimentary cocoa, welcome you with a smile, or give you a memory of a fantastic snowy day with friends.

When we become so glued to our computer lives, we often forget a world that needs a bit of laughter one can hear and not just a smiley face emoji on the phone.

When we don't pick up the newspaper and read its black and white print, we might miss a story that will cause us to smile or an obituary that will make us weep. Local newspapers are the heartbeat of a community that forms the bridge to connect us.

No, we can't return to the past, but perhaps the past needs to remind us that we could miss the opportunity to fly down a hill, scream with delight, and be on the front page of the local news if we don't take the time to look out the window.

True Leaders Carry Worn Bibles

A GIANT SOUL fell into the arms of God in February 2021. His passing was a consequential loss, not only for those who knew him well but because a good, godly man left this world. We need all the kind, godly people we can get around here. When God chooses to take the righteous home, I always pray another will attempt to fill those shoes, walk an honorable path, and become a giant.

Because of the on-going pandemic, his funeral was held virtually. I watched as the Methodist minister stepped up to the pulpit with a worn, broken Bible filled with letters and notes. I recognized it immediately.

The last time I'd visited my friend, Tom, and his wife, he was headed to Sunday school. He walked into the kitchen carrying his pile of lessons and the old Bible secured against his chest. I could not help but notice the Bible because it looked as if it might fall apart any second. It resembled a file that held everything from envelopes to scribbled notes and possibly a cookie. I never, for a moment, believed it would be the last time I had the honor of teasing him about hiding my pecan cookies that he always requested when I visited.

At the funeral, while we watched on the screen, the minister carefully opened Tom's Bible without disturbing its contents. Before reading a scripture verse, he quoted a statement by the famed English Pastor, Charles Haddon Spurgeon, which is so profound, I wrote it down.

"A Bible that is falling apart usually belongs to someone who is not."

The godly giant who leads an exemplary life continuously seeks truth and wisdom and becomes a leader for all. Thus, the best leader is the devoted follower of a mighty God. These disciples know to bow, weep, and pray for others. They are not boastful or proud; they do not use power to obtain fame. For the true leaders of our world, understand glory belongs only to a heavenly king.

When Jorge Mario Bergoglio became Pope Francis, one of his first acts was washing inmates' feet at a youth detention center. He became a leader yet understood he is merely a servant. He learned his role from the words of Christ found in the Bible.

"Your attitude must be like my own, for I, the Messiah, did not come to be served, but to serve, and to give my life as ransom for many" (Matt 20:28).

Tom's worn Bible was a symbol of where his earthly life was centered and a bridge toward eternal living once his mortal life was over. Here, his good life holds no candle to what awaited him because he believed in and trusted his Lord.

I recall years ago walking into Krispy Kreme near my house to pick up hot donuts for my Sunday School class. A man was standing beside me as the girl behind the counter loaded two dozen donuts into boxes.

"I'll bet you are headed to church with your donuts." He remarked as he watched.

"Yes, I am, are you headed that way too?" I replied.

"No, never. The churches are full of Bible-toting hypocrites." He espoused as if it was a fact.

I am not sure if I came up with the response or a Krispy Kreme-visiting-whispering angel was in line, but I immediately said, "Yep, you're right. But where else are we supposed to go to find redemption if not to God?"

He looked at me for a long minute, and then he smiled, as did I before I walked away. For some reason, that moment has stuck with me like glue.

The best way to serve God is to draw someone close to him by the example we set. We are not meant to be just readers of the Good Book; we are to use it as a guide to live. When we show love for one another, offer compassion, abhor hatred, and do for others we introduce strangers to our leader.

To think we know all the answers to life, quite frankly, is preposterous. We don't, and we never will. Tom's scribbled notes, folded up between the Bible's pages, revealed his continuing search for truth, for the right way to be the best example of living a life of faith.

We become discombobulated when we assume we are no longer servants. We lose our way when our pride and intelligence push us to believe in our rules more than God's laws. That never goes well; thus, we find ourselves being corrected and humbled.

Some of us stubborn souls need correction quite often. Or could it be our Bibles are just not worn enough?

In loving memory of Tom Mahaffey: 1940-2021

Leaving Age at the Curb

BEFORE CHRISTMAS 2018, I traveled with a group of girlfriends to New York City to see the bright lights, the holiday decorations, and, hopefully, a snowflake or two. Our spirits were high because our friend's niece managed the production of a little play on Broadway called *Hamilton* and we possessed priceless tickets. When we stood on stage and mingled with the cast of the famed musical, we were beyond excited.

Later we drooled as we gazed into the city's elaborate store windows, weaved our way through throngs of people, and relished each moment. It was the girls' trip right out of a movie. We never stopped whirling in the Big Apple until a group of young 20-somethings poured a bucket of sand in our boots.

We were about to step off a curb and cross the street toward a park when one young man hurriedly ran around us, cutting us off.

"Hey," one of his buddies yelled, "Watch out for the old ladies!"

Michele looked toward me, "Did he mean us?"

It pained me to tell her the truth, but since there were no other females of any age near us, I nodded to the affirmative. Michele turned pale, and the rest of us suddenly felt the need of a boy scout to help us cross the street.

In all the hustle and bustle of loving the city's vibrancy, we'd forgotten we were not those teenage girls starring in the movie. But suddenly we remembered we were all within a few years of reaching whatever age it is when youth is left way back yonder.

I love living in my own mind. I never considered myself old until I tried to apply makeup and needed a magnifying mirror to do so. Those lighted mirrors are evil! They also amplify those other travesties growing across your face that resemble a map with railroad crossings and warning signs.

It is funny how we view age as if it is something worthwhile to notice. So, perhaps we should not put so much effort into seeing it. My dad always said, "The worst part of aging is watching others who leave before they reach an older age." He was right about that because it sure is tough saying goodbye. For the ones who remain here longer, we should be celebrating each breath we take.

Shoot, I began writing at age sixty-eight: a new career, a new adventure, new friends, new dreams, and new deadlines. I am the new Grandma Moses; except I write instead of paint. And, of course, I am not famous. But, shoot, I might be! You just never know what is around the corner if you never give up trying ... and if you keep your spectacles on, so you won't hit a wall!

The world takes age way too seriously. Women, especially, take age way too seriously. We try to stop it, alter its looks, worry over it, and try to become who we once were in that old, school photograph. The truth is, we are basically the same people we were in school. The only thing that has changed is the photograph and, perhaps, our added wisdom.

Sophia Loren says, "There is a fountain of youth. It is in your mind, your talents, the creativity you bring to your life, and the lives of people you love. When you learn to tap this source, you truly have defeated age."

Words from a beautiful woman to those trying to turn back the clock when it is not time that ages us; it is our spirit.

Our spirits all suffered during the months of the COVID-19 pandemic, no matter what age we were. Some learned it is not our government or a vaccine that will pull us out of our battered souls, but it is up to each person to utilize every moment.

Staring at that mirror, or wishing for yesterday, or aimlessly worrying over tomorrow will age you faster than lying in the sun slathered in baby oil. There is so much more to life than worrying over something you cannot control no matter how much money you spend trying. Instead, take charge of making the world a kinder, less selfish place. Create warmth, bridge gaps, cause someone to smile, and suddenly age will be put in its place ... forgotten.

Take care of the body you have so that you can enjoy living in it. Your life is not over until they call your name from way up yonder. Did the good Lord tell you to sit down or stop? No. So, keep vibrantly moving and pour sand into the boots of those who step in front of you.

Live boldly, benevolently, and with God every hour of each day until you fly away.

For Broadway's southern girl, Holli Campbell

Friends, Golf, and Howling Winds

ONE SUMMER WE had the honor of visiting friends in Sheboygan County, Wisconsin. We traveled with seven other couples from Georgia who traded their flip flops and fans for golf shoes and cooler air.

This was my first trip to Wisconsin, except for traveling through Milwaukee on a train a million moons ago. I did not know what to expect from a state where the temperatures fall far below zero in the winter and where a cheese wedge sits on top of folks' heads during football season. However, to step off the plane and feel a cool breeze was just fine by me.

Rain began to fall on our way to Lake Elkhart Village from Milwaukee, and the activities our hosts had spent months arranging for us looked as if they might be washed away. After we arrived at the hotel and checked into our room, we headed to our friend's home a few minutes away. Smiles, hugs, bratwurst, cheeses, German potato salad, and all things Wisconsin met us at the door. The Midwest accent was tempered with a few *y'alls* and *bless your hearts*, plus the falling precipitation never dampened the spirits of this lively group of friends. Have you noticed that foul weather never rains on true fellowship?

When we awoke the following morning, the rain had soaked the earth. We thought we might need a canoe instead of a golf cart for our planned day of golf at a nearby public course. However, what was astonishing, was this group of sixteen donned their hats and rain jackets and proceeded to hit the links anyway. Since there were no paved cart paths, I navigated the terrain with my golf cart and did a few scary spins as we tried to brake going down a slippery hill or two. My friend accompanying me in the cart gave me a hug after one truly hairy ride and said, "Thank you for saving my life!"

By the end of the day, my socks and golf shoes were full of water, but would I trade the day for dry clothes? No, because memories are made from thrilling rides, daring souls, and crazy days.

Wisconsin is full of wide-open spaces filled with corn, red barns, silos, jersey cows, and green acres. There was a swelling sense of freedom when I looked across the non-cluttered, quiet, peaceful horizon where American flags flew above the land and lakes glimmered in the sun. Green Bay Packers tee shirts and hats were a wardrobe staple. Warm, soft pretzels, hot fried cheese curds, and cold beers were consumed by the pound, which kept folks fueled for the harsh winters. However, it was the friendly, smiling, easy-going Wisconsinites that added fuel to one's soul.

The Bull Golf Course was aptly named. Built on land, which was once a dairy farm, this course was challenging even for the finest golfers. Let me assure you, this girl was not anywhere close to fine. Plus, when The Bull blew thirty-mile-an-hour winds that tried to throw you off the tee box, it was incredibly tricky to hit a little, itty-bitty white ball! My girlfriends and I played together for our second day of golf, daring The Bull to chase us away. We laughed at the howling wind, applauded a long drive or good chip shot, and wondered why none of us could putt.

We hugged, high-fived, and tamed the bull. Isn't it true when you have good friends, the bullies are tamed?

Friendship is a beautiful, God-given gift we should be thankful for every single day. Whether we are having a golf day in the howling wind or when the winds of life toss us about like a twig, it is the friends who will calm the howls. It is those buddies who jump up and down when we achieve a goal and fall on their knees when we need God's help to stand. They are the ones that keep us traveling on down the road, together experiencing exhilarating adventures.

I have had the privilege to visit many states in my life. And from across this land, friends walk hand in hand under the same flag, the same sun, and the same stars at night. We can have differences, we can look, sound, and live differently, but one thing remains the same from the folks in Sheboygan County to every American acre: We all need one another.

The Evil Lurking in the Grass

THE YEAR WAS 1961, and my parents were building their dream home in Tennessee. Mother and I had driven to the new house to meet a contractor on a hot, August, Saturday morning.

When we arrived, saws were buzzing, and men with hammers were pounding nails into rafters. Mom, and the contractor tried to converse over the racket, and I strolled over to the vacant lot next to ours. A large oak tree on the far side beckoned me to come to enjoy her shade and quiet.

"Where are you going?" A voice startled me, and I quickly turned around to see a boy, speaking to me.

"I'm sorry," he said. "I didn't mean to make you jump!"

I met his gaze just as the sun caught the sprinkling of gold dust in his dark hazel eyes. His eyelashes curled up to his eyebrows, and his perfect teeth gleamed as he flashed a broad smile. He was stunning.

After introductions, we ran and played in the vacant lot until we tired. Then we sat under the big oak tree to talk. Henry was thirteen and the son of the nice contractor Mom was meeting with.

After a while, we headed back to the partially built house. Henry was a few steps behind me when he yelled, "Don't move, Lynn!"

I stopped dead still.

There was a large snake coiled in the tall grass in front of me.

Henry was able to calm me and keep my usual hysteria over such creepy, crawly creatures at bay, as he directed me where to step so I could get around the snake.

When we reached my mother, I told her about the snake, introduced her to my new friend, and the three of us walked toward our car.

We waved goodbye, and as we did, tears welled in my eyes because I instinctively knew I would never see Henry again.

"Why are you upset?" Mama asked.

When I told her why, she understood and said, "It is sad, but you are right; you probably will not see that nice young man again."

I, indeed, never did. Sixty years have passed and, yet I still recall the beautiful boy who saved me from the snake and talked with me under the shade of the oak tree.

Henry was African American, went to another school, and in the 1960s, it was often unacceptable to be close friends with someone of another race, or worse, to find them attractive.

I was born and bred in the segregated south, yet I never understood any form of racism. As a child, I remember thinking bigotry was absurd and wondered why folks judged people by the way they looked, the way they talked, or the color of their skin. I felt it was anti-God to do so. I still do.

Mama must have thought the same because I never heard her say a disparaging word about anyone. I recall this woman of few words, declaring once, "What's race got to do with anything? Whether a person is good, or evil doesn't have a thing to do with the color of their skin!"

Because this exceptional person was my mother, hatred and bias were not taught to me in words or actions. How grateful I am for her intelligence.

Do we really believe God judges us by the way we look? Or aren't we judged by the actions of our souls? What if God created humans of different ethnicities, cultures, and colors to enable us to see with our hearts instead of our eyes? What if He is giving us a big ol' test?

I know many folks who will need to go to summer school or be expelled if that is the case. There are people of all ethnicities who pass blame, resentment, and meanness down through many generations.

We ponder why there has been so much hatred, anti-everything in America. As I write this in 2020 White Supremacist groups, terrorist groups, anti-Semitic, anti-Latino, anti-Asian and anti-Caucasian groups are swelling. Organizations with messages that encourage hatred and violence.

Do they not understand they are hurting themselves, our country, and God?

Americans have made many steps toward equality since 1961, but there are still snakes in the grass waiting to cause harm, ready to upend strides forward, and ready to strike at common sense and decency.

To save us from their evil, may we all exhibit honor and kindness, so it shines like the sprinkling of gold dust in a young boy's eyes.

Lynn's Garage Gym

IF YOU WALK down our street on any Tuesday, Thursday, or Saturday, at 9:30 a.m., you will pass a house where the double garage doors are wide open. You will hear the Alexa Amazon Band playing various tunes from artists such as Michael Jackson, Maranda Lambert, or Bon Jovi. Such noise causes the dogs to bark and the humans to wear earplugs.

Folks hear the racket from far away and wonder why, in a neighborhood of mostly older people, such madness comes from the brick house on the corner. Then it dawns on them who the house belongs to, and it begins to make sense.

Yep, you guessed it, it is ours. After the gyms closed in 2020 due to the pandemic, I was determined not to be emergency airlifted to a hospital due to a chocolate chip cookie overdose. I needed to keep myself motivated to move and avoid such a fate. I took my tape measure to my small garage to determine the number of friends I could exercise with, while keeping safely spatially distanced. No more than five could participate.

Lynn's Garage Gym opened in March 2020, and it has saved a few of us from becoming slugs, sitting on sofas surrounded by Tootsie Roll wrappers. Every week I create exercise routines because boredom will surely kill any motivation.

The girls know if I am upset over some goofy government decision, they will need to do extra rapidly counted jumping jacks. When I am blue, they recognize that the ab workouts will be shorter, and the music will be a bit softer. But, when they hear Alexa belting Michael Jackson's *Beat It*, or, *Paradise City*, by Guns N' Roses, they know what they are in for.

My gym became official when Mr. COVID decided to stick around for a while. Even after some workout facilities opened back up, we older folks decided that it was not safe for most of us. One day, the girls surprised me with a custom-made, black, iron sign that reads between the molded weights, *Lynn's Garage Gym*. I adore that gift because even though it says, *Gym*, the garage has become much more.

We say prayers on days when the world outside the open doors seems bleak and dark. We wave at the neighbors as they stroll by smiling at the crazy ladies who believe they are still only seventeen. We rarely fully agree on politics or the breaking news, but we never let it make a difference in our friendships.

Many days we go over my weekly newspaper column, and I receive constructive, honest feedback. We complain about the ugly rolls of a mysterious entity on our bodies that never seem to go away, yet we are grateful we are still around to see them. We long to hug our grandchildren and gather at friends' tables, but in the end, we are thankful we have each other and the gym.

I can tell when one of the girls is down or tired, so I crack my whip harder, and the blues seem to float toward the sky. We laugh when a bird decides to fly into the gym for a visit, or when a stranger almost runs over a mailbox when he hears moans and groans along with Amazon's Alexa screaming the lyrics to, *Pink Cadillac*.

There is much to be said about finding motivation amid sorrow. It is so difficult not to succumb to the doom and gloom. We bemoan the loss of ordinary days and long for their return. Would not that be wonderful! However, there are a few things I hope we never do again.

I hope that we nevermore return to ingratitude. I hope that we have learned that complaining is quite useless and that prayer is quite essential. I hope we forever remember that life can change at a moment's notice, so that we enjoy every moment of even the most mundane days.

When I watch my workout sisters as the sweat pours off their brows, I witness abundant life and relish health in our little gym. I do not take breathing or friendship for granted, and I pray none of us ever will again.

We find we are stronger when we exercise, not just from the weights we lift but also from the mental strength to weather life's hardships together. Our power comes from having the endurance and courage to survive the worst of times.

The adage, "What doesn't kill you makes you stronger," is appropriate. We finally recognize that strength comes from our hearts, not our muscles. Ultimate, lasting power only comes from love, kindness, empathy, and gratitude for God's abundant blessings.

On the Wings of a Sparrow

SUSAN AND I were living in the same suburban Atlanta subdivision in 1988. I, along with other mutual friends, would often attend neighborhood parties with Susan and her husband. Niceties danced around the room to the beat of the music as chatter filled the air. Susan and I were merely social friends until the music stopped for both of us.

By 1991, her husband had passed away, leaving her with two teenage boys to raise. I, too, was a single mother after a long relationship.

The good Lord blessed two weary souls when He found a way to bring us together. I can't explain how we became close friends, but we grew to be each other's tear stoppers, soul bearers, and comrades in a war to regain our emotional footing.

Susan was Michigan-born and bred, brilliant, elegant, and tactfully direct. This southern gal is none of the above, and when folks noticed our friendship becoming stronger, they would often produce a furrowed brow in wonderment.

One April evening, we were on our way to our favorite restaurant when Susan complained about a recurring pain in her side. I encouraged her to see her doctor immediately.

By the following week, she was diagnosed with incurable liver cancer. She died just a few months later, in July. The last words I said to her as I left her house the night before she passed away was, "By the way, Susan, I love you!"

My unlikely soul sister was gone. However, because of her influence, I didn't fall apart; I instead jumped into action. I knew her extended family was in Michigan, and it would be a day or so before they arrived. I needed to help her college-aged boys navigate the world of funeral preparation.

The boys and I planned the services, and friends prepared the house for guests. When the minister came to discuss the ceremony, he asked what hymns the family would like to hear.

Because Susan loved gardening and found such solace there, *In the Garden* was chosen. There was another song she adored, but none of us could recall the title. We told the departing Reverend we would soon let him know the second hymn.

Throughout the day, while absorbed with sadness and planning, we kept trying to remember the song.

One of Susan's sons developed swimmers' ears, and early the next morning, I headed to the nearest pharmacy to get ear drops before heading to their home.

I was in the pharmacy one minute after the doors opened. Quickly, I picked up the necessary medicine and headed toward the cashier. A woman who had been jogging was checking out. While waiting behind her, I noticed her earphones loosely dangling from around her neck. I could hear the faint sounds of a hymn I recognized. Chills formed over me as the cashier said to her, "I love that song! It's *His Eyes are on the Sparrow*, isn't it?"

As I walked out into the bright July sun, I smiled because I absolutely knew Susan was alive and well. *His Eyes are on the Sparrow* was the song none of us could recall.

By the end of the day, the family had arrived, and the minister had all the necessary information. On my way home, I suddenly realized I did not have a summer dress for the funeral service where I was to give a eulogy!

The malls were about to close, so I quickly drove to the closest one. After trying three department stores, I walked into a dress shop, exhausted.

Susan loved navy blue linen and hanging on a sale rack was the perfect navy linen dress. Sadly, they did not have my size, so I took two others to the dressing room. All six cubicles were empty and cleaned, but I chose the second one to my left. Once I closed the door, I saw hanging on a single hook the same perfect navy linen dress in my size.

After the family returned home and the boys headed to college, I went to the cemetery and laid a blanket down by Susan's grave, where I finally wept.

A gust of warm air blew the tree branches above me just as the sound of a multitude of sparrows flew from the mighty oak and scattered into the summer sky.

Folks often question and forever will if there is life after death. I never do.

In loving memory of Susan Kane: 1941-1995

The Spirit of the Fallen Soldier

IT IS DOUBTFUL anyone loved their country more than the fallen soldier. He was the warrior who one day walked onto a battlefield with a fierce determination to protect and defend his beloved America, only to never return to its shores. Not including the Civil War, we have lost almost seven hundred thousand service members on battlegrounds because of such courageous love.

These soldiers were born into families that were of different religions and different ethnicities. They were Republicans or Democrats or neither. However, on the battlefield, it mattered little because they were all in the same mud, the same trenches, experiencing the same horror and fighting together to save their country. They gave their lives to defend equality for all, for freedom to worship, and for Americans to have the freedom to speak and vote.

Courage has no color and no voice. Bravery is born of the heart, which believes there is no greater love than a person laying down his life for another. We need to look no further than the seven hundred thousand graves scattered across this world to see headstones depicting such love.

My daddy always said, "When our country starts losing its way and folks no longer take pride in America, that is the day war will begin, or a tragedy will occur to wake up the spirits of the fallen soldiers. That is the day we become unified. Our backyard debates and political party arguments go silent. We all realize at that critical time what matters most is saving the land of the free."

When my father was around thirteen, his widowed mother ran a boarding house near Jamestown, Tennessee. He was the youngest of four children, and he regularly helped his mama with the chores and duties of running the inn.

"Ray, you need to go to the train depot in the car to pick up Sergeant York and take him to his home," she yelled from the kitchen, one day.

Yes, she was speaking of the same Sergeant Alvin C. York, World War I hero and recipient of the Medal of Honor and numerous other awards. In 1927, most thirteen-year-old boys knew the story of the famous Tennessean who stood exposed to gunfire from German machine gunners atop a hill in northern France. Nine of the seventeen men in his unit fell as a barrage of bullets tore through them. Quickly, York led the remaining soldiers in a charge to attack the hill. Being an expert marksman, Sergeant York silenced thirty-five machine guns and took 132 Germans as prisoners.

Also, in 1927, if a thirteen-year-old knew how to drive a car, he took the wheel. As Ray inched toward the train station, snow began to fall in Jamestown. Undeterred, as soon as the Sergeant got off the train, the boy proudly saluted him.

Ray Walker drove a hero eleven miles to his farm as the snow started to settle on the roads. When they arrived, the Sergeant stepped from the car, telling the lad to come in from the cold.

As the snow and ice accumulated, Sergeant York sent word to Ray's mother, Rose, explaining why her son would stay with him until the weather cleared.

It took nearly four days for the roads to be drivable. During those days, the Sergeant told stories about the war and his service to the awestruck young boy who would later become my patriotic father.

Daddy always declared that when Sergeant York talked about his infamous battle, he spoke with deep sadness about the comrades he did not save on the hill that day in France. The Sergeant was a renowned hero, yes, but within his heart, he remained a man without pretense or pride and humble enough to make sure his new young friend was safe.

Gary Cooper won an academy award for his portrayal of this remarkable man in 1941. After Alvin York received all the fame and accolades, the ailing Sergeant tried to enlist once again to fight in World War II.

Perhaps if each American paused to remember folks like Alvin Cullum York, or the seven hundred thousand soldiers whose remains lie over battlefields around the world, we might become a more grateful, thoughtful nation. If we teach our children the personal tragedy of war, they may come to understand the importance of peace.

All fallen soldiers have a story to tell of their heroism. They came from all corners of these United States and gave their lives for us. It is vitally important to keep telling their story because we might garner enough courageous love to heal a divided country if we listen.

Do we need war or tragedy to unite us again, or might we learn a valuable lesson from the spirits of our fallen American soldiers?

Salute the Vietnam Warriors

WHILE THUMBING THROUGH my old high school yearbooks one day, tears pooled in my eyes.

They were all there, young men with hope in their eyes and their youth on the edge of disappearing. What would they have accomplished in their lives if they'd had the promise of a future?

Would they have laughed, as I do, at the silly antics of a grandchild? Would they still possess the impish grins the camera caught in the 60s? Maybe Howard would have made it onto the big screen with his good looks. Perhaps Bobby would be a renowned physician today, and Larry might have climbed the ranks in his beloved Army before retiring to Florida.

However, the maybe's left when they boarded a military bus and headed off to serve our nation while the war escalated in Vietnam. They, like so many, returned only to be laid to rest in their hometown cemeteries. Laid to rest before they had a chance to see what could have been.

These young men joined the service, as so many do, to become soldiers of war. They were the elite among us who, I believe, God anointed with an extra dose of courage. They went bravely into battle to defend the land they loved.

They steadfastly looked out for each other and often gave their lives to save their comrades.

The Vietnam warriors were no different in character and honor from those who bravely fought for our independence. They held the same gritty spirit as those who battled before them in the Revolutionary War or World Wars I and II. But the warriors of Vietnam did differ from the soldiers in previous wars. The soldiers who returned from Vietnam bore a scar.

By the time our troops were pulled from Vietnam in 1975, over fifty-two thousand young soldiers had perished. Between 1964 and 1975, 2,709,918 men and women wore an American military uniform in Vietnam. 261 of them were awarded the Congressional Medal of Honor, as Bobby Ray was, for saving many lives, except his own. Of those killed in combat, sixty-one percent were younger than twenty-one. Just out of school, just beginning to dream, just starting a future.

Also, in 1975, America's electorate was deeply divided. Some say the military was demoralized. So, for those who returned from the rice paddies and trenches, from the ships and the skies and prisons of Vietnam, there were no homecoming parades or bands of screaming, happy folks in Times Square to greet them. Vietnam was simply over for America.

Today these fallen soldiers are immortalized on a wall in Washington, D.C. For those with loved ones whose names are etched in this wall, the war is not forgotten, nor is the sacrifice. We are the older generation now, looking back at the young, innocent faces in our yearbooks. Our faces bear the lines that attest to the joys and sorrows of living long. Their faces remain ageless.

Today, six hundred ten thousand courageous Vietnam Veterans still walk among us. Of those who risked their lives in Southeast Asia, ninety-seven percent were honorably discharged even though many were drafted to serve.

Even after countless acts of heroism and bravery shown by our American troops during the second-longest war in our history, they returned home to be treated harshly by many for just doing what they were asked to do. Unfortunately, this response caused much grief and created a loss of self-esteem for many young soldiers, and it led to deep-seated problems.

Our worst divisive behavior is the scar of Vietnam. The wound was not caused by the soldiers. The injury was inflicted by the free citizens who remained on American soil that turned their anger toward those sent to battle.

We can fairly charge those in government for almost anything, but we ought not charge the bravest, the best, and the most elite among us. We should never blame the warriors—the ones who suffer and give the most. Nor the hundred and fifty thousand who were wounded in Vietnam, nor the prisoners of war, nor those missing in action.

I look into the eyes of the framed Vietnamese doll my brother sent me in 1965. She has my POW/MIA bracelet around her waist to remind me of another pilot whose remains were finally located a few years ago. My brother lived until 1998, but his time spent in Vietnam was always fresh in his heart. I, too, vow to honor those who gave so much and received so little.

Let's remember the brave soldiers of yesterday who gave up their tomorrows so we could live today. Let's celebrate their short lives.

Maybe it will help heal the scar a divided nation caused and remind us never to produce such a wound again.

"It is foolish and wrong to mourn the men who died. Rather, we should thank God that such men lived." ~Gen. George S. Patton, Jr.

Fiery Trials

Tragedy, destruction, sadness, and evil cross our paths during our lifetime. None of us are immune from the heartache these fiery trials cause.

To survive, we need to wear the armor of God and be thankful He supplies such bravery. With His help, we learn to face fear, understand more, and show others the power of courage.

Never give up even when sorrow and pain surround you. Your life is worth the fight.

"God is our refuge and strength, a very present help in times of trouble" (Ps 46:1).

Secrets Behind Pretty Picture Windows

AS AN INTERIOR Designer for over forty years, I walked through the doors of many houses, and I know within the walls of most homes are hidden secrets.

I met Mary when I first began my design career. She called the office and set up an appointment. A week later, I pulled into her driveway. Her house was a modest brick ranch with a carport attached. A large picture window graced the front next to the entry door.

Mary's welcoming smile illuminated a pretty face with dazzling eyes. After introductions, she explained her sister was getting married. Mary wanted her home to be in perfect order for the bridal parties she planned to host.

She was a corporate nurse and a young mother to a cute-as-a-button, three-year-old girl. I immediately bonded with this lovely, young, spirited woman.

"I've never had draperies on this big window, and I finally have enough money saved to have them custom made. Could they be finished before the first bridal shower?" Mary excitedly asked.

It was the '70s when swags, cascades, and sheers were the rage in window treatments. They were expensive but the height of style in those days. I thought they were a little over the top for her modest house, but I sure did not want to tarnish Mary's dream.

I designed them with a casual look, and Mary adored the fabrics we selected. After the drapery installation on a Thursday, I phoned Mary to see if she was pleased. "Oh, my gosh, Lynn, they are fabulous! I love them!" She shouted as I heard her little girl calling, "Mama," in the background.

The following Sunday, while drinking my coffee, I read the headlines in the local paper. Seconds later, I dropped my cup.

Mary's little girl found her mother lying in a pool of blood on the kitchen floor on Saturday morning. The murder was a result of multiple stab wounds. The little girl's father was under arrest.

In my first meeting with Mary, I recalled asking her if her husband liked the idea of new draperies. "Oh, I am not going to tell him! He bought a new car, so I am getting window treatments with my savings."

Could draperies have sparked rage? Probably, but I know with certainty, resident violence hid in the little house behind the pretty picture window.

Ten million people per year are victims of domestic abuse. Unfortunately, Mary was not the only one I would meet living in horror behind their front doors.

One of my clients was thrown from her three-story home's top balcony yet survived after days in ICU. Another, a school Principal, lived in fear because of a verbally abusive, dominating husband. A lovely physician finally divorced a physically abusive spouse after her last stint in the hospital.

All the above were successful independent women who suffered one day too long, tried one too many times to work things out, until the one day their lives shattered because of death or injury at the hands of a *loved* one.

After my divorce, I began dating an old friend. He came to my home for a dinner date one evening. My eleven-year-old son was in the kitchen as my friend walked in. A quick spat developed between my date and me because he was not only late but reeked of alcohol. Suddenly, with violence, he grabbed me from behind, jerked my neck to the left, and then threw me across the room. I hit the wall with a resounding thud before landing on the floor.

I saw stars but immediately gathered myself because I knew I must protect my children. With adrenalin pumping, I picked up this 6'2" man and threw him into the garage. I passed my small son, who was violently shaking, standing in the kitchen holding a large butcher knife.

I hugged my child and whispered, "Son, that will never happen again!" Today, when my neck pops and aches, it is a reminder of an evening long ago when I refused to let abuse take up residence in our world.

Secrets hidden behind the welcoming doors of a home can quickly turn into terror. There are countless reasons folks stay in horrible situations, but there are no good ones. Our homes are to be our sanctuary, and our loved ones should protect, defend, and live in harmony with us.

As I write this today, I see sweet Mary with her illuminating smile standing over my shoulder wanting to encourage all who live in chambers of violence to get help immediately. Our children deserve to have sweet dreams of peace and wake to see the dazzling eyes of their mothers.

National Domestic Violence Hotline: 1-800-799-7233

Clouds of Destruction

THE CLOUDS GATHERED quickly, filled with doom, and darkened the sky. I stood on the back porch of our middle Tennessee home in the early '60s, watching the trees sway in the wind.

I had witnessed intense storms before, but this one was bizarre because when I glanced toward the front of our house, the sky was a light, odd, pinkish color.

"Mama, come here!" I yelled from the back porch as the winds became more violent.

"Let's get to the basement!" she exclaimed once she viewed the forming funnel cloud heading our way.

The tornado skipped us that fateful day, but the folks just south of us were not as lucky.

A few days later, we drove to the area where an exquisite historic home had once stood majestically among acres of hardwood trees. I could not believe my eyes! All that was left was a toilet! The twister downed the mighty trees or snapped them into twigs. The home's residents were spared because they had gathered in the small powder room under the stairs where they, and the toilet, survived.

I was born in Putnam County, Tennessee, about twelve miles from where, once again, this time in March of 2020, the unfortunate wrath of Mother Nature rained devastation down. She took families, homes, animals, and trees, leaving nothing but tears in her wake. How quickly life can change. How rapidly we can go from sweetly dreaming to begging God. How swiftly our security can be tossed to the wind.

As I write this, pangs of guilt stab me as I am basking in the warmth of a Saturday morning, with the sun beaming through my office window. I hear the faint hum of electricity as it flows to lamps and computers. I am surrounded by papers, family photos, books, and my old Bible. And, as I write these words, I am aware that all I see could be gone in a split second.

Each time a tragedy strikes in our world, there is a part of us that is both thankful and mournful. We pray and mourn for those who have died due to Mother Nature, disease, or violence. There are more of us who are good people who sincerely care for others and try to do what is best rather than not. However, the one thing we are all guilty of is *distraction*.

We will go on about our lives, play our games, meet our friends, laugh away the day, and quickly forget others' suffering because we are not experiencing it ourselves.

We do not live in an area that is decimated, nor are we the ones who will bury a child or a grandchild. We will wake up to another morning sun, fight over politics, complain about our bad backs or our bad luck, and not remember how fortunate we are.

We become distracted by our abundance instead of being attracted to another's needs.

After Hurricane Katrina devasted the Gulf Coast in 2005, my husband and I traveled to New Orleans as quickly as possible to see what was left of his family's homes. The closer we got to the Mississippi coast, the more the landscape changed, going from green to nothing. From Heaven to Hell in mere miles.

Katrina destroyed an area the size of all Great Britain. To this day, down the streets if you look carefully, Katrina still holds court.

My life changed once I viewed such wrath. I realized life and all I know could be gone within moments. I understood with a new clarity that children could be taken from my world, that disease could befall me, and that Mother Nature could visit my back yard at any moment. I am not immune to tragedy.

Once we understand our shared vulnerability, the less we are distracted by silly stuff, which in the end is meaningless. What is meaningful and valuable is our compassion, kindness, and giving hearts.

My family has roamed the hills of Putnam County, Tennessee, for over two hundred years. They cultivated the land, built their log cabins, and tamed the wilderness. Determined Tennessee folks will rebuild, and one day a sense of normalcy will return. However, they will never forget a sleepy morning in March 2020 when the clouds rained destruction, and their world changed.

And, neither should the rest of us. Be thankful for all you have and give all you can to those who lose so much.

The Hallowed Halls of Democracy

OPINIONS AND THEORIES about the events of January 6th, 2021, have been plentiful. Blame has been passed around like the mashed potatoes on Thanksgiving. However, one aspect of that Wednesday we all agree on is that it should never be forgotten.

For the better part of my writing career, I have tried my dead-level best to promote kindness and understanding. When I write, I always envision God as my boss, whispering, "Write from your heart, write healing stories, and weave them around my teachings."

Sometimes I fail, but I sincerely try.

Most of the time, I have steered away from politics, except to calm the reader or encourage each person to view the other side. My best friends know where I stand on many issues, but publicly promoting my personal views was never in the best interest of all.

One of my editors questioned me one day. "When you write about our political environment, how do you seem not to offend either side?"

My answer was, "I am just trying to heal a big ol' divide I feel is dangerous."

Our country has endured so much since its birth. And in the 21rst century the threats seemed to accelerate. In 2020 far from having 2020 vision, we seemed to be blindsided each month by some new disaster. We attempted to hide from the coronavirus, inflaming political ads, and increasingly elevated racial tensions. The virus and politics dangerously mixed, with people fighting over the efficacy of mask-wearing, the skewing of statistics, and truth of science. Blame, distrust, fear, and vitriol swirled in a kettle, becoming hotter and hotter, until we could almost feel the sting of a burn.

Fingers pointed, friends fought, and enough tears fell to fill buckets. Yet, there was not enough weeping to put out the fires burning in our cities. People endured so much pain to prove their positions and declare their patriotism was greater than their neighbors'.

Soon after dawn broke on January 7th, 2021, people posted on social media their theories on who was responsible for the assault on the US Capitol. Who turned the protest into violence? Conspiracy theories reached a new low without basis in fact—simply full of rhetoric.

Just a few hours after being sincerely frightened with the uncertainty of who had broken into our nation's house, Congress stood together and declared, "This must stop!"

What was true then, is still true, today. It's easy to accuse a group with whom we do not align—blaming them for the hatred, for the anger, for the violence. It's harder, but worth the effort for us to shoulder our share of the blame.

Hate, anger, ungodliness, and evil climbed those Capitol stairs in 2021, and we were all responsible. Every person who spread hatred and bias, walked the steps.

Patriotism is not found in our souls' harshness but in the depth of our hearts. It is caring enough about each other to not tear down but to build up. It is not condemning someone's vote, but in the glory of America's freedom to cast a ballot.

Democracy thrives by finding common solutions and walking to the compromising table together before giving up. It is not sparring and fighting in our individual, selfish, deep-seated corners. It is not pointing fingers.

In 2020 we lost over four hundred thousand citizens to COVID-19. They should have been our unifiers. Their voices should have risen from every grave and shouted, "Stop the madness and help each other get well!"

But their muffled cries were drowned out by discord among those living. Their lives were reduced to percentages and numbers because our compassion failed.

I pray every citizen will put the swords of conflict and animosity away. Honor our veterans, our forefathers, and our children by being good, decent people. No good comes from being boastful Republicans or Democrats. If we want our country to survive, we must be Americans first and foremost.

We must heed the calming voice of the Almighty, who pleads with us, "Will you please, just love one another." It is God's words that will douse the fires of hatred and honor the hallowed halls of Democracy.

Miss Carter's Green Pastures

FIVE HORSES GATHERED at the fence behind the barn waiting for Miss Carter to bring them treats. She patted their noses, told them they were each special, and she would return with more love in the afternoon. Apple, the young colt, tilted his head as Miss Carter whispered to him as only she could do.

Afterward, Miss Carter returned to the barn to prepare tea and cookies for friends joining her for a picnic.

Miss Carter is three years old; the horses are seven inches high; the fence is constructed of popsicle sticks, and the barn is made of plastic. This idyllic scene rests on a child's table in my living room. However, for Carter and me, our imaginations allow us to travel far. We visit places where there is the freedom to ride, climb trees, and play in a hayloft.

I am called Grandma by this spirited, sweet child. We are not blood-related since she is my stepdaughter's little girl, but never mind all that. Family dynamics are way too complicated for a three-year-old. Love seems to cancel such trivial nonsense anyway.

Carter broke her femur in a freak accident at her preschool several weeks ago. She looks exquisite in her pink and purple Spica cast, which begins just under her breastbone, travels down her right leg to her ankle, and the left leg to her knee. A steel bar is attached from the right ankle to the left thigh, which separates her legs by about two feet.

She cannot walk, nor can she sit without assistance. She sleeps only on her back because she cannot turn. And she sleeps like this without complaint. She requires constant supervision, and when she needs to move, we must lift her, including the heavy apparatus she is half-buried in.

I keep Carter three days a week since she cannot return to school until the cast is removed. I have learned to sit with her around her table in little chairs that rise one foot above the floor. As a result of the lifting and sitting, I take a substantial amount of Ibuprofen for my back on a weekly basis.

When we are not at the barn, we go to Barbie's house, visit the girls, or shop at the grocery store where the head cashier, Miss Carter, runs the Minnie Mouse cash register. We unload our groceries in the kids' kitchen and prepare cookies containing pretend ingredients of vegetable soup with cherries. We solve puzzles, and without cheating, I cannot win a game of Candy Land to save my life.

In her infinite wisdom, Carter has taught me a lot about life during these last few weeks. I realize if I were in her situation, the claustrophobia would have set in, and my wailing would have spooked all the horses, causing them to flee to greener pastures. I would require more than Ibuprofen to get through the days, and not even Godzilla could lift me since I would have drowned my sorrow with real cookies made with chocolate chips.

Children are amazing. They accept what befalls them and roll with the punches. They use their imaginations to escape to bliss and enjoy the love showered upon them as they go. They choose not to complain but instead hold their dolls or bears and, if need be, watch Alvin and the Chipmunks to ease their burdens. They do not worry too much about tomorrow because they assume it will eventually arrive, bringing a new horse to the barn or more folks to the tea party.

Adults could learn a *tractorful* of insight by observing God working through a child's mind and soul. I understand these terrible things happen to even the smallest of humans since we live on this earth. However, when they do, because the children are innocent, God calms their soul and I think he must whisper to them, just like Carter does to her little colt, Apple, to assure him all is well.

When tragedy visits us, perhaps we should remember that courage will help us stand again. Miss Carter understands that attitude makes a huge difference in how we heal. We can choose to laugh at Alvin and the Chipmunks or cry and complain over our misfortune. We can decide to pray to God or blame Him for our troubles.

Children trust us to make things okay. They believe our words of comfort, "It's going to be alright." Are we not God's children? If we believe in His words, everything will be okay, even on the day when the horses come with chariots to take us home. Until then, enjoy the green pastures, let your imagination fly, and appreciate the love bestowed upon you as you go.

The Pink Sunsets of October

WHEN I SAT in the dental hygienist's chair, she attached what I call the "bib" around my neck as they all do. The paper bib was adorned with a scattered pattern of pink breast cancer ribbons.

I had been so consumed with worry over COVID, wildfires raging through the western states, political upheaval, and protest … but looking at the bib, the pink ribbon startled me. My thoughts flew back to October nine years earlier when my daughter celebrated her thirty-eighth birthday.

The family trip was planned to coincide with her big day. We all gathered at the beach, where we rented a house to accommodate a slew of folks. I have a photograph of her hugging her six-year-old daughter as the coastal sunset threw a pink cast across the beach behind them. It is one of my favorite pictures, but like many snapshots, it comes with a story.

Earlier that day, shortly before the photograph was taken, I walked into the bathroom, where my daughter had just washed her hair. As we chatted, I noticed strands of blond hair lying over a good portion of the cold white tile. My heart jumped with alarm as I grabbed a cloth to wipe them up.

"Guess it's time to get my head shaved, Mom." She announced with such resolute calm, the lump in my throat disappeared.

"Unless you want to keep cleaning this mess up, I would say you are right!"

We both laughed a bit, but to this day, I still get a lump in my throat when I think of that October evening.

When I see pink ribbons, a jar for donations at the convenience store, football players wearing October pink, or anyone who is in the throes of chemotherapy, the heartache is just beneath the surface of my soul. For me, it is a reminder of a disease that attempted to take my precious child from us.

There is an old saying that pretty much applies to many life events, "You don't know anything about it until you have lived through it." The *it* can be a disease, poverty, hunger, or racism. The *it* can be what it feels like to lose your home to a fire or a hurricane, lose your loved one to suicide, or lose your job because of a killing virus.

I certainly never knew what breast cancer could do to a family. I had read about it, but I did not understand the despair, the uncertainty, or the raw courage it would take to withstand such pain. I watched as my child underwent a year of physical struggling and fighting to return to wellness.

We do not understand until we have lived through it.

It has been nine years, but I still recall the medical teams, the doctors, and the nurses who compassionately walked with us through 2011 and 2012. I vividly see the chemo room where women gathered with their magazines as they watched chemicals slowly flow into their bodies. It was as if they were casually sitting under a hairdryer at the salon. However, worry, fatigue, and desperation were hidden behind masks of raw, unadulterated bravery. I was astounded at their sisterhood, their spirit, and their determination.

No, unless you have been through it, you do not understand. Nor would anyone who has experienced such grief want you to. However, we must recognize that even though we may not have endured such pain, we must have empathy. It is compassion for others, the gifts to others, the desire to help another that will heal us all.

There are so many who are living through extreme heartache this year. The year that I write this. The year that you read it. Breast cancer and other cancers will continue to claim lives, and so will diseases, fires, illnesses, accidents, and violence. For those families who are grieving and struggling to survive, trust me, they need our aid not only in prayers but also in donations and tangible assistance.

My adopted hometown in Georgia is like the rest of small-town America. As I write this my town is reeling from dropped income because of the pandemic and watching as friends and family suffer. But LaGrange citizens still have the town square wrapped with a vibrant pink ribbon around its perimeter. The fountain in the center rains droplets of pink water. It is a beautiful sight to behold, and it brings hope home. Storefronts put pink ribbons on doors because there is compassion for those who suffer. Theirs is a reminder that the *it* can always happen to those who once simply did not understand.

Many diseases have no cures, but donations and prayers get us closer to one every day. Give what you can to those who are living only to see a pink sunset once more.

Mending the Broken House and Heart

WHEN I WAS a little girl, my friend Martha owned the prettiest doll-house on the planet. Lucky Martha was an only child whose father managed the local five-and-dime store in town. Naturally, she would have excellent toys!

There must have been some magic at Martha's house because to this day, I still recall her enchanted dollhouse—the one I longed to call my own.

Several years ago, I decided, since Santa never brought me a dollhouse like Martha's, it was high time I should own one. I purchased a kit, built it piece by piece, shingle by shingle, and donated it for a charity auction. My dollhouse raised a significant amount of money for Breast Cancer research, so the dollhouse magic continued.

I never dreamed I would attempt such a feat again, but a broken dollhouse landed in my lap. A family member received a tattered, hand-me-down house for her daughter, but it was too much for her to repair.

"Lynn, since my daughter has a newer dollhouse, would you like to restore an old one?"

After she sent me a photograph of the house, I reluctantly said, "Well, okay, I guess. Bring it over."

The large, two-story, pink house sat in my office for months with its broken door, missing shutters, broken bits and pieces of furniture, and mismatched walls. Each time I glanced at it, sitting in the corner, a wave of sadness crossed my heart.

When I finally began the process of restoring the house, my husband asked, "What are you going to do with that old thing when it's finished?"

"I'm not sure, but I will probably donate it to a charity around Christmas," I answered with a total lack of enthusiasm.

The more the house began to transition to a home, the more magic started to return. Room after room became its own sanctuary with hand-sewn tiny pillows, braided rugs, art, and window treatments.

Each area from the nursery to the kitchen enjoyed a touch of Christmas with red, green, white, and black splashes. A Christmas tree adorned the living room, complete with miniature packages waiting to be ripped open. A white cake with red berries sat on top of the stove to cool while tiny coffee cups rested on the breakfast table.

"Now, what are you going to do with this?" My husband asked again as the dollhouse neared completion.

During the long hours of restoring the old house, I envisioned a little girl seeing it for the first time. Every stitch, and with every stroke of paint, I saw a child's face and knew it was to belong to one little girl whose belief in love and hope needed mending.

My friend, Michele, is a volunteer for CASA. They are the initials for Court Appointed Special Advocate for children. These extraordinary volunteers and leaders represent children from broken homes placed in foster care. These are children who have suffered from abuse or neglect. They are in need of a voice in court to tell their story. They are the innocents who need to be kept out of harm's way and guided to a safe and productive future. CASA becomes the protectors for the girls and boys whose hearts are broken and who require healing from their worlds' harsh reality.

"Michele, do you know a little girl in need of a special gift for Christmas?" After Michele saw the house, she took pictures and sent them to CASA's local office. The CASA teams carefully researched to find the unique child who longed to find a glimmer of hope and belief that Christmas is magical.

Michele and I loaded the house into the car and took it to the CASA office. I was pleasantly surprised to meet many CASA leaders who came to see the mended home. Pictures were taken as I told the dollhouse's story and told them about the little girl, I envisioned receiving it.

Without divulging too much information, they explained, "We have decided it will go to a young girl and her little sister who we felt were the children who would best benefit from this gift at this time."

Months earlier, I purchased a family for the dollhouse as an extra present. It included a mother, father, a little girl, and her older sister.

I smiled as I looked at the dollhouse for the last time. The old, neglected house was restored to its original beauty. There is hope in everything broken if only we take the time to mend them. However, the real magic lies in the CASA teams and the countless volunteers who work tirelessly to protect over four hundred and thirty-five thousand foster children whose dreams are broken.

What better way to restore Christmas joy in our country than to rebuild hope in the heart of a child?

The Ones Who Missed the Dance

A WARM OCEAN breeze swayed palm trees as we drove west from Pompano Beach, Florida, to the resort hotel where we were staying for the weekend in March 2019. My granddaughter would be involved in dance competitions inside the hotel crowded with costumes, chatter, devoted parents, and nervous performers of all ages.

I try to miss none of the significant events my precious angel deems essential. Her fourteen-year-old Pompano toes have been tapping to the beat of the music since before she was age two. So yes, this was a "Grandma flying Delta" worthy occasion.

As we drove toward the Coral Springs resort, the landscape transformed into streets lined with sidewalks framed in manicured perfection. Gated communities protected exquisite homes where residents walked dogs, biked, and jogged with friends. Flowers bursting in blooming color flourished under the bright Florida sunshine. As the sun melted into the horizon, a pink hue was added to an already peaceful, quiet portrait of stunning.

We made a right turn toward our hotel, and I saw a large, well-landscaped school adorned by a distinctive entrance. The institution's name was proudly displayed on a stucco facade: Marjory Stoneman Douglas High School.

Yes, we were in Parkland.

It was Friday evening, and all the students were busy with their lives somewhere other than on these grounds. The Eagles' home was silent as if it were just another school building waiting for bustling activity to resume on Monday.

However, there isn't another school quite like this Parkland school anywhere. There are few schools in our country whose names evoke every emotion from love to hate, but to stand physically before this pristine white stucco structure takes the viewer beyond the headlines and the horror.

Beneath the school's impressive entrance lay a portion of earth covered with a multitude of flowers. Above the bed of colors rose seventeen illuminated angels representing the seventeen lives lost on Valentine's Day 2018. Three adults, six sons, and eight daughters left for school one morning and never returned home.

As we drove by the stone gates in upscale communities, many still hoisted large banners: "MSD STRONG. Our home. Our family. Our community."

We should consider it necessary to put the same banner in front of our homes no matter where we reside because Parkland, Florida, is a member of America's community.

However, our sense of connection can be lost when we become so quick to turn a tragedy into a political nightmare. Without thinking of parents, students, teachers, and those innocent lives lost, we can distance any and all emotion for the sake of professing our political affiliations and beliefs.

Two more students plus a grieving father died from suicide in the aftermath of that Valentine's Day massacre. The people who walked those halls and witnessed such horror were never going to be as they once were before that fateful day. Grief counseling would be a part of Marjory Stoneman Douglas High for a long time.

Until we address the severity of stress, bullying, and mental illness thriving in our youth, and the insensitivity in our adults, we are likely to see more angels rising from the earth.

After the tragedy, I was amazed by how many people sent hate mail and showed disdain when several Parkland students protested for better gun laws. What a tragic example of how unempathetic our community's citizens can become when we allow our political views to take precedence over compassion and kindness.

Whether one believes the students were right or wrong, their fight came from young souls trying to heal and make a difference.

As I watched my ballerina angel twirl across the floor amid hundreds of other young dancers, I thought about those missing the dance. I wondered about Alex, Cara, Gina, Alaina, Luke, Jaime, Martin, Nicholas, Helena, Joaquin, Carmen, Peter, Alyssa, and Meadow. Not so long ago, their little toes were also tapping to the beat of the music at age two, but they will never dance again.

At times, we must put away our differences and not turn every situation into a political or affiliation-based debate. We should show others that compassion, understanding, unity, and love can rise above ugliness. We must bind together to protect the innocent, our children, by becoming more thoughtful than we currently are and by providing a better sense of community in America. It is way past time.

Perhaps then we would be as Marjory Stoneman Douglas High, "America Strong. Our Home. Our Family. Our Community."

Someone Other Than Me

I WAS DIAGNOSED with clinical depression many years ago. My doctor treated me with therapy and counseling for over twenty years until one pill a day entered my life and saved it. I was one of the lucky ones.

My depression began when I was in third grade. Instead of being me, I wanted to be the girl with the shiny blond curls seated next to me. She was smart, pretty, and happy. She was only the first of many I longed to become. I never liked being me. If someone teased me, I wept for days. If a bully was mistreating someone else, I cried for the underdog. When I failed at anything, it was because I was undoubtedly a complete failure.

Suicide entered my mind many times, and at one point, I attempted it. I am brutally honest here because there is no reason not to be. Becoming transparent is how we help those who suffer and who wish they were anyone else but themselves. Depression creates pure hopelessness, and life is viewed behind a veil of sorrow and gloom.

In 2020, multitudes were hurting. Because of the pandemic, daily doses of death, isolation, and loss of income and normality played mental havoc. Suicide, depression, and anxiety rates rose. No one was immune from the sadness of that year. The virus brought with it the harshest of stings, and its poison affected us all.

However, for those who were already enduring depression, it was far worse. One day, in the middle of that hard year, the blue depression monster jumped in front of my computer. I was preparing to write my column, but as I stared at the blank page, my first thought was, "Why?"

Why was I writing? The world was sick and angry. Pessimism had risen to a new level, and those hard-headed, political, name-calling, divisive folks were driving me crazy! When I went to a store that required safety protocols and noticed a customer stroll by with no mask, who seemed to not care about others, they caused me to question the world's fate. So why write? It was hopeless. Why talk about the kindness and goodness of God? It is hopeless. Why write about love when such selfish hate seemed rampant? Why?

I wrote a note to one of my editors. "Is it time for me to put the pen down?"

Then, as if a magic-wand of reason were waved, a reader emailed me after reading a recent column, "Keep writing and being the voice of love and peace. You are deeply appreciated." This reader had no idea I was ready to quit.

The blue monster faded away, words formed on the blank screen, and the hand of God calmed my soul. Once we recognize our purpose, we become what our creator intended us to be. Hopelessness fades to bravery, death fades to living, and we accept who we are and why.

When we deliver unselfish, caring behavior to others, we become instruments of service to all. Those who watch the world through the fog of depression and only hear the angry and judgmental voices lose confidence in living. God really does want us to care about other people. He knows those who grieve, and he calls on all of us to render aid.

Everything we do is visible. When we promote negativity, we damage. We whisper, judge, and wonder why folks would die by their own hand. Yet, we never ask ourselves if we had a hand in their death by taking away their faith in mankind? Has our self-indulgence prevented us from hearing the cries of those who have experienced profound loss? Are we guilty of spreading doubt, hopelessness, pessimism, or rage?

For those of you who are suffering, who would rather be anyone else but you, I urge you to hear my words: **There is no one better than you.** Each person was made by God to fulfill a mission. Today, you may not know what your mission is, but one day it will become crystal clear. Do not buy into the messages given by the world's bullies, the naysayers, and the name-callers because they do nothing except hurt. You must never believe there are no good, decent folks bearing kindness, compassion, and love left because there are. These are the folks who heed God's explicit instruction to "love one another."

Do I still wish I were someone else? Some days I do, but I also realize if I were someone else, I might not be strong enough to fight for those who want to be someone other than their valuable selves.

National suicide prevention hotline: 1-800-273-8255

Live to Hear the Birds Sing

THERE IS A BIRD singing just outside my office window to interrupt the silence surrounding me. The coffee is still warm enough to drink, and I should eat a bit of breakfast, but the thought of food doesn't appeal to me. The sky is gray, and the floor around my feet is cluttered with items I should pick up.

I put on gym clothes this morning but doubt I will exercise unless I take a long walk. If I do, I plan on walking alone. I am questioning why I write and why I am here. Why does life seem distant today, as if I am not quite up to living?

Deep in my mind, I know the answer and the battle I will need to fight to enjoy the little bird's trill fully. I have walked back into the shadow of depression. I suppose this depressive episode will not last long because I have the tools to combat it, unlike those who do not recognize its call to isolation.

Even though I take a daily medication for the illness that has affected me since I was in elementary school, the shadow can be triggered by the simplest things or a variety of what I call "add ups." Those are the petty annoyances that have accumulated and become one major headache or heartache.

When I awake with feelings of insignificance, exhaustion, isolation, or not wanting to converse, then I know I have some work to do. When my friends tell me I look tired, or they ask, "What's wrong?" I am aware my depression has risen to the surface.

I share my brief walk with the shadow while knowing others live with depression symptoms every day behind closed doors. They never hear the birds singing or have friends who remind them, "something is wrong."

There are sixteen million Americans who have experienced or are living with major depression. Some, like me, will battle with clinical depression for most of their lives. Most of these folks will not seek help. Many don't have the means to pay for medical assistance or can't find affordable facilities offering support. Some will commit suicide, others will turn to alcohol or drugs to numb the pain and they will slowly, daily wither away.

Van Gogh, Michelangelo, Sinatra, Springsteen, Lincoln, Churchill, Beyonce', Bon Jovi, Hemingway, Rowling, Winfrey, Parton, Bradshaw, DeGeneres, and Mark Twain are just a few of the hundreds of well-known people who have battled major situational or clinical depression. Depression does not care if you are famous or not, nor does it care about your age, race, or religion. Like most illnesses, it requires medical attention, and many will seek it; but many can't or won't.

People have asked me why I am so open and transparent with my readers. There is an answer, and it lies with sharing life with my sweet mother.

She was the most reserved, quiet, and intelligent woman I ever knew. She never shared her personal struggles, nor did I ever witness her succumb to emotion except when her father passed away suddenly. She was never judgmental and could always see the other side of someone's story. She had only one fault that I am aware of, and it was her fear of allowing those she loved to witness any of her weaknesses. Many times, I felt I did not know her even though I adored her.

It was common for her generation to hide those things which are unpleasant and painful. I remember, on one occasion, after a severe bout with my depression, she handed me a gift. The present was a framed quote from a famous poem called *God Always Sends Rainbows After the Rain*. It was one of the few times we openly discussed *sadness*.

After she died, when I stood next to my mother's grave gazing at the flowers surrounding her, I was happy she was now filled with joy in heaven. At that moment, I understood she, too, had lived with a sadness she could not express or reveal out of fear we would learn just who she was.

Our desire to remain anonymous as victims of depression hurts not only us but also others who share our world. We must speak about our own battles with mental health to encourage others to seek aid and open their locked doors.

God helps! Lord, does God help! He encourages us to live every day to the fullest. God wants us to be the best we can be to fulfill his purpose for us. He begs us to seek and see the rainbows after the rain.

I feel a bit better now. I will pick up the clutter, listen to the bird's singing, and watch for the sun to break through the gray.

No Matter What, Give Thanks

ON FRIDAY, THE 13th day of November 2020, someone famously, sarcastically exclaimed, "What could possibly go wrong?" Even though it elicited laughter, the truth is, most of us recognized we might want to avoid stepping on cracks in the sidewalk, breaking any mirrors, or walking under ladders. Because 2020 had been a tough year.

We were fatigued from worry, sadness, and in many cases, loneliness. Many had lost loved ones due to the pandemic, and others had lost jobs and income. We had suffered the slings and arrows of a bitter, contentious election that disrupted many relationships and hardened our hearts.

Then, it seemed as if the COVID Grinch was trying to sabotage our traditional, joyous holiday season. What else could possibly go wrong? None of us would have been surprised if there had been a turkey recall or a limit on yams or cranberry sauce the week before our 2020 Thanksgiving!

So, how were we supposed to elicit gratitude around our Thanksgiving tables that year? How were we to we find happiness amid such sorrow? Where did we toss our bitterness, division, and heartache?

The answer was found in one word: God. We can all say we believe in a higher power, we can all attend religious services, and we can all tap our prayer emojis on our phones, but there are times we are each called to "use" our faith.

When we face daunting hardships and seemingly hopeless tomorrows, we can either succumb to defeat or turn to our faith. The Bible tells us to give thanks in all circumstances. My take on that is we are to find gratitude amid a pandemic—amid loss, uncertainty, and insecurity.

A good friend of mine was shocked by the sudden news of a possible cancer diagnosis. As I held her while tears ran down our cheeks, I found myself extremely thankful that she is a part of my life. God gave us many years of love and laughter, and I prayed there would be many more. However, I was thankful that she was blessed with the personality and strength to forge forward and fight. She would *use* her faith to travel the rocky road she was to navigate.

There is a reason to be grateful in every situation, even as tears fall and life is upended. Perhaps, we just need to recognize the gems hidden in the tragic times.

We fight over politics and elections, stomping our feet and gritting our teeth. Yet, we raise our flags and take pride in our country, calling it the land of liberty. God gave us a gift in the men and women called to service. They maintain our freedom, allowing us to openly pray to Him. Our hearts should be filled with gratitude even as we stomp our feet and grit our teeth.

As a pandemic swept our world and fear gripped our souls, there was much to be thankful for: The doctors and nurses who risked their lives caring for the suffering. The grocery clerks who stocked our shelves and the farmers who supplied our food. The first responders who rushed to our aid and the scientists who strove around the clock to find cures and treatments. So many people were diligently working; the least we could do was be thankful.

Often, I question why some folks do not have faith. If they study and contemplate the diversity of the individual skills we possess, they might change their mind. If we were all born to become doctors, then who would put out the fires? If we all were meant to be firemen, who would cure the sick? The vast network of talent and skill knitted together for mankind's survival was not generated by a computer but by the hand of the Divine.

There is a moment for gratitude in every situation. When we can see the light of God cut through uncertain darkness, we discover hope.

That Thanksgiving in 2020 did not resemble a Norman Rockwell painting for most of us. In my house we turned to the guest seated at the head of our table and, with a resounding, heartfelt shout, we exclaimed, "Dear God, thank you, for you! Thank you for being with us—for teaching us that trusting you is how we find gratitude, joy, and peace. It is how we love, how we forgive, and how we forge on with strength. Your grace and mercy are immeasurable. Please help us to believe that in all circumstances, we are to give thanks for the blessings you bestow upon us."

The COVID Grinch tried to sabotage the holidays, but nothing could steal our hopeful joy when faith provided us with grateful hearts.

The Healing Power of Appreciation

IN 2020 WHEN much of the country was isolating due to the COVID-19 virus, we gathered for an outdoor visit with a few spatially distanced neighbors. We sat under the oak trees and laughed with friends about silly things, as people do when they are tired of the news, the heartaches, and events in our world.

At 7:14 p.m., we collectively prayed that our country would be cured of the horrific disease that had trampled our lives and disrupted our world. Don, my hometown friend, requested that we raise our voices at a specific time to fill the heavens with healing pleas. I so appreciate the friend who reminded us of God's words, "For where two or more are gathered in my name, I am there among them."

Afterward, friendly chatter filled the balmy air as nature came alive with its own pleasant noises in the twilight. But within the hour, the wholesome sounds of crickets and frogs in competing cacophonies were drowned by the sound of sirens rushing into our neighborhood.

My husband had collapsed. A strong, healthy man who had laughed in the moonlight just a few moments before, became eerily quiet. His color began to return as the paramedics attended him, trying to determine what was wrong.

The ambulance drove him to the emergency room to make sure he had not suffered a heart attack or stroke. Because of the pandemic, one could not accompany a patient to the hospital, so I remained on the phone most of the night with those who were attending him.

The hospital was full of newly confirmed coronavirus cases, and after David had a thorough check, it was determined it was safe for him to return home. As I drove the deserted highways at three o'clock on a Wednesday morning, I realized how much I appreciated the paramedics. How thankful I was for the doctors and nurses who aid any who call for help. How grateful we were that my husband was coming home when I knew others that night might never return to their families.

David would follow up with more tests, but as of right then, he was back to his boisterous self, yet a bit altered. He realized that one could be transported to a world of uncertainty, doom, or death within a moment.

We all take life for granted most of the time. It is not until we realize it can be taken away that we start appreciating every breath we take.

The following dawn, while David slept in, I turned on the morning news. Those dreaded increasing numbers popped up on the screen, recording rising coronavirus deaths and hospitalizations. We viewed the same statistics every morning without much thought as to what they represented.

Every number was a person who was sick or dead. They represented heartache and suffering. Behind each digit was a person who felt fear, uncertainty, solitude, and pain.

Webster's dictionary defines the word appreciate as "to grasp the nature, worth, quality, or significance of ... ."

The appreciation of life is essential to obtaining compassion, grace, and understanding. If one is grateful for nothing, then what is their nature or worth?

Our dear friends spent their summers in the north. They were careful, took all precautions, but from some unknown source, they contracted COVID. Typically, they would have been under the oak trees on a balmy summer evening with us, but not that time, not that year. Instead, the normalcy of life was completely taken away and replaced with debilitating sickness. When David was rushed to the hospital, our appreciation of their lives intensified, and our daily prayers were filled with asking God to heal our friends.

David's seventieth birthday came. As he blew out the candles on his cake, I snapped a photo. His daughters were beaming as the flames illuminated their faces—a snapshot of life, love, and happiness.

How grateful I am for the man I realized was not as safe and as carefree as he once was. How thankful I am for the living love of those who surround me.

When we value others, we realize we must do all we can to protect them. We should pray in multitudes. As I write this, we are still in the middle of the COVID pandemic. You may be reading these words after this pandemic has passed, but there will be more trials to come. And when they come remember: We need to take necessary medical precautions no matter what any politically based group might say. We are not merely numbers; we are humans who can lose our lives if we do not treasure every person's life.

Let's all band together and appreciate our days. Let's live them abundantly and serve others, and may God be among us as we do.

Those Tumbled-Down Days

SOME DAYS, LIFE seems to take a tumble, a misstep, or it feels as if something is just plain off. Days when our energy is low, but our worry is high. Frustration, sadness, and fatigue sink in, and we wonder why.

Most of us want to go back to bed, cover our heads, and pray that tomorrow will be an *on* day and our joy will return. However, I believe we need those troubled days to recoup, rethink, and redo. Perhaps they are given to us to settle ourselves, be alone, and even shed a few cathartic tears.

It has been said that writers pen their best works during episodes of depression. I'm not sure how that works when you are buried under the covers, but the idea is plausible. Depression and art often go hand in hand. From Van Gogh to Hemingway, those tumbled-down days gifted the rest of us with beautiful words and breathtaking paintings. Their talent rose to the surface in the quiet moments of loneliness and disillusionment.

Recently, I was experiencing an *off* Tuesday morning. Too much to do, worry, and a lack of sleep threw me for a loop. I received an email from a gentleman after he read his newspaper earlier that same day. He wrote, "Your column this morning is just what I needed to face a grueling day! Thank you."

How funny that his note helped me face my own grueling morning with a new resolve. And that, my friends, is how life works. Life flows better when we realize we all need each other to survive our tumbled-down days.

While on vacation, my sweet friend fell and broke her foot. This is not the first time she has broken a bone due to a tumble, so I knew she was frustrated. When she sent a message to all her friends telling them of her accident, her phone lit up with good wishes! By the time I talked to her, that little cheery, laughing-at-herself attitude was again in full bloom. We definitely need one another to heal from all falls.

Years ago, before emails and cell phones, I wrote my mother a letter after a crazy day with my new baby and a mischievous toddler who persisted in providing trouble. I comically explained the entire day but ended it with the word, "HELP!"

Mom called me after receiving the letter a few days later.

"Honey, I am sorry you had such a terrible day, but I laughed until I cried as I read your story."

"Gee, thanks Mom, I am glad I made your day happier from my misery!" I kidded.

Then she thoughtfully responded, "Lynn, you really can write, you know."

I replied, "Mom, now you are the comic!"

When I was going through Mother's papers after her death in 2010, I found that old letter and, in my grief, a much-needed smile crossed my face. She had helped me indeed.

When nothing is going our way, and when life seems complicated, and trouble lurks, it is usually a signal for growth. In our solitude, we find we may need to reevaluate our priorities, pray a little more, or even pen a novel.

It is a monumental struggle to find strength and meaning during our dark times, but it is worth a mighty try. Perhaps, in the end, you could discover that your darkness created light for someone else. And that, in turn, motivates us all.

One of the most significant faults human beings have is our inability to call for help. Our pride gets in our way, and fear of what others think of us rises above what is best for us. Here's the deal, every single person on earth always and forever will need aid at one time or another. No one is immune from down times and arduous journeys.

The trick is how we manage them. Do we go to bed and hide, or do we face struggles head-on and grow from our down times? If you look straight into the eyes of God, He will tell you to get up and do no matter how you feel. Ask for His aid, call a friend, or seek wise counsel. Out of the darkness, Van Gogh painted A Starry Night. And, out of lonely silence, Hemingway wrote sentences that echoed around the globe.

Never fall from tumbled-down days, but instead, see what beauty you can create from standing tall through them. When you do, you just might help another not to tumble.

Faith

My faith is the cornerstone of my life. As I look back on my years, I know it was the Lord who often lifted me from despair and cured my weary heart.

It was the hand of God who blessed me with my family, friends, and all the gifts of my life. I earned nothing; He gave me all.

God's words whisper the stories I am to write, and as I watch them turn to print, I am humbled.

For me, I will stand before the cross, praise His holy name, and bow with thanksgiving till the day I see His wonderful face.

" 'If you can?' said Jesus. 'Everything is possible for one who believes' " (Mark 9:23).

Life Beyond Grief and Sorrow

HE LEFT THE lumber mill he owned accompanied by his beloved dog, Snowball. They walked the usual path around the small fishing pond, which sat peacefully between his home and the mill. It was lunchtime, and he knew his wife, Nannie, had his hot cornbread waiting on the table with fresh summer vegetables. He closed the screen door and went to the powder room adjoining the kitchen to wash his hands. After a few minutes, his wife began to call his name, fearing the cornbread was turning cold. When he did not respond, she found him lying still on the powder room floor. On August 4, 1965, a man quietly moved from a busy, bustling earthly life to heaven within mere seconds.

John Alexander Pugh, my seventy-two-year-old grandfather, was a formidable, robust man who left his family and community in shock and grief.

My grandmother was inconsolable.

Death can arrive abruptly with no warning, no chance to say all those things we intended to say yesterday, which makes mourning more difficult. I overheard folks at his visitation say, "I saw John the other day, but I didn't have time to stop and chat." Or "I meant to take a trip to see him this summer but got busy." Regret accompanies death most of the time in one way or another, and for some, it never goes away.

I was seventeen and preparing for college when my granddaddy died. Early, on the morning following his death, I walked out to my grandparents' carport and found my father weeping.

Without taking his eyes off the mill sitting silently beyond the pond, he whispered, "John was the only father I ever knew, and I loved him."

I wondered if he ever told his father-in-law the depth of his feelings.

My grandfather's death taught me valuable life lessons. I watched as folks came in and out through the screen door bearing food, flowers, and memories. I grieved with those whose love spilled over this remarkable person who touched so many lives. My heart broke as I saw my usually strong mother consumed with weakness, when she realized she would not have one more conversation with her father.

I felt my grandmother's pain and saw raw emotion as I had never before witnessed it, and I learned in those days what faith can do.

Granddaddy was a deacon in his church, and he loved God. There is no question where this honorable, faithful servant is today.

My grieving grandmother finally started to see the sun again on a day when her eyes indeed saw that death is not the end.

She told the story many times in the years after.

She would walk the mile to the cemetery to visit her husband's grave several times a week for months following his death. Each time during her lonely trek home, she would be drenched in tears and covered with sorrow. One day, in the distance, she saw her husband standing on the sidewalk with his hands on his hips, appearing very upset.

She knew it was a strange vision, and she rubbed her eyes to erase the anomaly. However, as she proceeded toward the image, the clearer John became.

"Nannie, what are you doing going to visit me at that grave and getting yourself all worked up and sad!" He emphatically asked.

He continued, "You know I am not there! Use your faith!"

The vision abruptly left, and soon, so did the tears. Nannie knew where John was and used her faith to inspire so many, including me.

That is what believing in, and trusting in, God can do. With faith, you can hear the voices, see the visions, and experience healing relief.

At seventeen, I learned folks need one another when grief comes calling. Those cakes, casseroles, and condolences are brought by friends to ease our burdens, to show their love, and offer aid any way they can.

I learned to share and be open with my feelings today because I am painfully aware, the people I need to tell may not be there tomorrow. I am a big believer in all kinds of reunions because I do not want to miss seeing a beloved friend or family member who may not attend another one.

Yes, death will arrive, but it is not the end; it is just the end of this journey. I have endured the deaths of many loved ones and will experience its sting again. However, life continues beyond the tomb of grief, pain, and sadness to a place where we never will endure such sorrow again.

If only we believe.

The Music Just Beyond the Doors

SHORTLY BEFORE MY mother passed away, she described a vivid dream she experienced one night that prepared us both for what was to come.

In the Tennessee mountain town where she and I were born, the vacant old Imperial Hotel stood frozen in time as if passing years dared not touch it. The brick, three-story building next to the train depot was built in 1909. Weary rail passengers would enjoy a good meal, then relax, before bed, in the rocking chairs on the balcony, feeling the cool air as it whirled around the mountain. The Imperial boasted thirty rooms and indoor plumbing, which in 1909 was quite extraordinary in the hills of Tennessee.

When I was a small child, the old hotel was a magical place where I could imagine myself as a traveler on the Tennessee railway or attending a gala in the main ballroom. However, in the late '50s, the passenger trains redrew their routes and no longer dropped travelers at the depot just below the hotel. As a result, the Imperial closed its doors to guests, and silence filled the halls.

The once-thriving resort town and tourist destination withered. All other inns and hotels succumbed to the ravages of time. But the Imperial stood fast, determined not to be forgotten. It was as if she was still waiting to greet her visitors when they walked through her doors once again.

"Lynn, I dreamed I was at the Imperial last night," Mother told me one morning. "I was in the foyer hall alone, and the doors to the ballroom were locked. I heard a band playing and people laughing as if they were attending a fine party. I wanted to join them, so I knocked and then banged on the old wooden doors. The noise inside grew louder, and my attempts to be heard were useless. I began to weep with frustration because I desperately desired to see everyone, but I could not. I woke up this morning with the dream still fresh and found my pillowcase was damp with tears. So strange."

When Mother passed away a few months later, we took her home to the little mountain town to rest beside Dad. A day after the service, I drove toward the Imperial and wondered if I could somehow get inside. After parking my car, I found, to my surprise, the front door was unlocked, and I discovered I was alone in the building.

Old wooden doors were open to reveal a large room perfect for hosting a huge celebration complete with a band. But unfortunately, the hotel was void of sound. Yet, I could feel the beat of the music as I envisioned my parents dancing as they always loved to do.

While standing among the spirits still alive in the Imperial, I understood how Mom's dream prepared us for her departure from this world. In the end, Mother was ready to join the others who waited just beyond the doors to eternity. Her frustration was over.

We are sent images and messages of eternal life all the time. Either we decide to pay attention to them or ignore them completely. Usually, when we don't trust what we hear or see, we deem ourselves more intelligent than the Divine, proving that we aren't really very intelligent after all.

People call these images and messages different things. Some call them God-Winks. Other say they are bizarre coincidences or even hogwash, but I call them gifts. Precious connections to unite us with God and those we have lost from this life. They remind me of a small present tied with a satin ribbon. Once you untie the bow, the box reveals glimpses of forever.

Today, the depot near the hotel is a museum run by its cultural administrator, a young man new to the area. Mr. Cleary fell in love with the town's history and the under-three thousand people who call Monterey, Tennessee, home. I met him for the first time when I visited a few weeks ago.

He had just purchased his first house.

"Where is your new home?" I asked. After a brief conversation, I knew exactly where it was.

It was the house where I was born.

I looked up to the hill just beyond the depot to the old brick Imperial and smiled. There was no music flowing from the rooms, nor sounds of laughter, nor trains that stop to deboard weary travelers seeking rest. Yet somehow, the magic that makes life whirl like the wind in the mountains reminds me that we all remain connected to the past, to those we love, and not even death can stop the dance.

Sometimes, when we are caught up in the noise of life, it is vitally important to become quiet and listen to the music just beyond the doors.

Where Did God Go?

AS THE LEAVES began to pale and clutter the ground, I was reminded of my childhood days. In the Tennessee hills, there were plenty of fallen leaves around by October. No matter how much Dad would rake, gathering leaves into piles, the yard was never cleared. Plus, my friends and I raced to jump into those mounds of color as he grumbled his way through the chore.

Once the trees were bare, we all knew the holidays were just around the corner. Mom would start planning early, as I do today. I noticed she spent more time at her sewing machine and studying recipes. There was a sense of anticipation when the cool air became cold, and kids everywhere prayed for the first *big Tennessee snowfall.*

It is the simple pleasures we once enjoyed that captured our hearts. Life's little joyous moments fill our minds with a longing, a desire to return to a time when the world seemed safe, carefree, and filled with wonder.

In fall, perhaps it is good for us to just be still and watch with fascination as a leaf falls to the ground. As I write this, in 2020, we are living in challenging times filled with uncertainty and angst. Two hundred thousand people will not be joining us this holiday season. There will be empty seats around tables at Thanksgiving and for those of us who are still here, there may be no Christmas gifts. Many have lost their businesses, jobs, or homes.

This autumn, we find sadness in every corner and anger rising to a new level. We are consumed with politics. We cannot make a cup of coffee without it becoming political. Friends ostracize friends if they disagree on issues. There has never been another time in my life that I have witnessed such a prevailing spirit.

We are dealing with so many complicated, controversial problems, it is overwhelming. They can overtake our spirit, cloud our perspective, and diminish our faith. We may ask, "Where in the world did God go?"

The truth is God has not gone anywhere, but perhaps we have. Have we lost our way with our sorrow, our hopelessness, our anger, and let the state of America today cloud our lives? Has our spirit fallen like the faded leaf that wearily drifts to the ground?

I would say the answer is, "Yes, we have." The only true healer of our spirit is our spirit. Our relationship with the Almighty is what will motivate us to mentally recover. Perhaps, God is reminding us that He alone is in charge and is watching how we handle diversity and a complex, contentious autumn.

Folks worry and fret but forget the word of the gospel, "Do not fear, I am with you." Our brothers and sisters spew hate and spread evil like wildfire and forget the gospel's great commandment: "Love one another as I love you."

God has not gone anywhere. Perhaps he is watching us as we turn away from Him. We will not recover if we do not turn around. Faith is the most essential medicine we have. It is not found just in words or our sermons, but in our individual actions.

Today, as my own spirit wanes, I recall those days when Daddy raked the yard, and Mama sewed my Halloween costume. I believe we can return to those joyous times, but only if we turn toward God so that our deeds will be filled with godliness. Empathy, kindness, love, goodness, and faith are the medicines we must take—the medicines prescribed by our greatest Healer.

We must never forget that we cannot outsmart God. We are not that intelligent; we are not that righteous; we are just merely mortal humans. God is not the president, not a congressman or a Superior Court judge, but He alone is the supreme being who will decide our fate.

Yes, God is still in the yard, but just blurred under the leaves a bit. He is still the one who will be praised at Thanksgiving, and of course, Christmas is His celebration. Let us honor Him with our actions, and maybe, just maybe, we will heal our hearts and our country when we do.

Take a moment and notice a leaf cascading to the ground because the wonder of life is found in such simplicity.

When Most Fear is Gone

AS I AGE, I realize with gratefulness, fear of most things seems to be gone, except for my fear of snakes. If I live to be older than Methuselah, I will still be afraid of those creepy, crawly critters on my last day.

During our lives, we all endure moments of terror.

Several years ago, I was on a flight when the plane abruptly dropped in the sky, causing drinks to fly to the ceiling and eliciting screams from passengers. The young man sitting beside me turned to me after the jet decided to remain airborne and asked, "Ma'am, I fly often, and that took my breath away with a bit of fear. How did you stay so calm?"

I thought about his question a moment before I answered, "Well, I am not sure, but I believe it has to do with trust and faith. After living through tragedies plus many trials and tribulations, I realize I made it through them all, usually finding it was for a reason. So, why be afraid, except for snakes. One should always remain cautious of those squirmy slitherers! Have you seen that movie, *Snakes on a Plane*? Now, that is my idea of fear!"

He roared with laughter as those around us wiped spilled coffee and dried their tears with paper towels.

When I was young, I was fearful of many things. I remember being terrified that death would take away my parents or my brother. I feared monsters in the closet and zombies on television. Storms didn't scare me until I saw a tornado turn a house into toothpicks.

When I became a mother, fear for my children became constant. I tried not to worry, but a mother always does. When they all began driving, my heart would race as if I had seen those snakes on planes! And, when I watched them fly off into the world, my worry was only calmed by praying for them to have a safe and joyful journey.

We go through life with fear by our side. What will tomorrow bring? Who will leave without saying goodbye? When will it be my day to bid farewell? However, we must never let fear become the focus of any day.

It is suitable for us to be cautious in making decisions and always wise to look for snakes before stepping blindly into a forest. A dose of fear can keep us from doing dangerous, dumb stunts. However, when fear paralyzes us to the point of not trying new, exciting adventures, then we need to seek the counsel of the Wise One.

I was playing golf yesterday with good friends. I am not sure how the conversation started as we walked off the last green, but our friend, Mike, made a startling statement, "Take the fear out of your problems."

How many times do we put off solving a problem because we are afraid of the results? What if we fail? What will folks think of us? The key to solving an issue is taking the fear out of the problem to view a solution. Isn't it better to try and fail rather than not try at all? Not trying is a failure. We can find the necessary courage to solve a problem when we seek the counsel of the Wise One.

My father was in the hospital many times during the last few years of his life due to congestive heart failure. One Monday in November, he was admitted again with the same symptoms. His mood was upbeat, causing all the nurses to laugh at his shenanigans. By Thursday, we all knew Dad's heart would not allow his witty ways to continue.

"Dad, are you scared?" I asked with tears brimming my eyes.

I shall never forget his response, "What is there to be scared of?"

A few hours later, the angels took him to meet the Wise One, who had replaced his fear with faith.

Looking back upon my years, I realize that I did survive the death of my brother and parents. The fear of life without them was replaced with the courage to live. I found those monsters never came out of the closet, and I still have not encountered a zombie. My children continue to drive cars, and I pray that they arrive safely and avoid those snakes hidden in the grass wherever they go.

I listened when the Wise One said, "Fear not, for I am with you. Do not be dismayed. I am your God. I will strengthen you; I will help you; I will uphold you with my victorious right hand."

And I believed Him.

My Father's Way

MY FATHER IS the best! He will not be with me on Father's Day because he resides in heaven. However, he remains in my soul. I can say without hesitation that without him, I doubt I would have survived these many years.

He gave me a manual long ago, which was my life's instruction book. Often, I ignored it and created my own rules. It never works out well when I decide not to follow instructions. After falling and failing many times, I finally perceived that my father is smarter than I am.

I looked at the old instruction guide the other day and saw many of the highlighted sentences which Dad asked me to honor. *Love* is marked with a pink highlighter. In my early years, I understood love was the ingredient needed to experience a good life. At first, I thought it meant the way Mom and Dad cared for one another, but as I grew, I understood that love in abundance thrives when you love others as yourself. Dad said, "Love isn't selfish; not to be hoarded, but unselfishly shared." The more love we give away, even to those who are enemies, the more love we receive.

Dad was right. But he always was!

Forgiveness was highlighted in yellow. Father always said, "You must forgive those who hurt you." Lord, as many times as I disappointed Dad, he never seemed to change his affection for me. He always forgave me, would hug me, hand me his instruction book, and tell me to study. Forgiving ourselves and others clears our path toward wisdom.

Resentment and anger do not allow us to experience joy. My father was right about forgiveness. But he always was!

If you wanted to make Dad angry, you just had to be judgmental. If I showed arrogance or acted as if I were better than another, my father put me in a corner where I wrote, "Judge not, lest ye be judged," about a hundred times. He could put me in shame quicker than my grandmother, which was quite a feat.

Grandmother always taught, "Walk a mile in another's shoes before you judge them."

Dad would add, "Yes, keep walking in those shoes, or I will add rocks to yours!"

Now, when I see arrogance and judgmental behavior in another, I know they are walking with rocks in their shoes. Eventually, they will fall, so I guess Dad was also right about that!

How many times did I hear my father say, "Trust me!"

"Well, how am I going to fix this, and how am I going to survive that?" I would ask.

His response was always one word, "Faith." Then he would add, "Little girl, you have to keep your faith to see the unseen."

When I was little, I was confused by the *faith* verses, highlighted purple in my book. How was I supposed to see something invisible?

One day I thought, well, I do not see air, but I know it is there. I cannot see love, or hate, or angels, but I know they exist. So, I guess Dad meant that you must trust those things which live in your soul to help you survive the *this and that* of living. Faith is like a life preserver when we are drowning, and hope is the gift faith brings.

The longer I breathe, faith becomes the air; I could not live without it. So, my father was right about trust. Of course!

I am a bit sad today because I think my brothers, sisters, and I have neglected Dad's instruction book. If we read it, we will become less angry, more open, kinder, and compassionate. We need to implement the highlighted words and listen carefully to the voice he left within our hearts.

Yes, I had, and still do have, the best father in the world. He goes by many names, but my favorite is God. His instruction manual is the Bible, and we are all his children.

To you, Father, the one I trust, the one I love, the one who holds my hand, and the one who puts me in a corner, I say, "Thank you."

Happy Father's Day, my Father. I love you, Lynn.

PS: God, please thank my earthly father for introducing me to you.

Cling to What is Important

IN MY LITTLE office, one will find family photos amid papers, books, disarray, clutter, and chaos. This morning, I was feeling a bit exhausted, and all the mess seemed to overwhelm me. Ribbons, paper clips, pencils, and pens somehow flew to the floor, and how did all the pictures hanging on the walls become crooked? Did we have an earthquake only in my office?

As I study this catastrophe, there is one item on the top of a dusty bookshelf that puts my soul at ease. It stands a mere seven inches tall and four inches wide and always speaks volumes to me when my eyes locate it among the rubble.

One of the Mahaffey brothers from my hometown presented it to me as a gift. It is hand-carved from wood, a bit rustic, but lovely.

A note the artist, Don, wrote on the bottom reads, "Thank you, Jesus," the date, and then, "Representing the Power of God." The little carving always reminds me that I should "simply to thy cross … cling."

How many times do we become overwhelmed by life? We all get sidetracked, fall backward, stumble forward, and create a bunch of clutter as we go. We cause misses, messes, and mayhem. Afterward, we wonder how we will clean up the debris left by our actions and continue to crawl through life.

My grandmother always said, "The world is full of sinnin', and the only thing that'll set us straight is simply to cling to the cross."

Many times, it is hard to find what is vital amid the shambles. For those of us with even the tiniest amount of faith, eventually, the cross will rise and beckon us to embrace the power of God.

When my son was a toddler, I would sing him a tune while cradling him in my old rocking chair as it creaked and wobbled just like my voice. It is a wonder he survived the utterly terrible racket of both. There were two songs that he repeatedly would ask me to sing. One he called "Mace Grace" (*Amazing Grace*) and the other, "Cross" (*The Old Rugged Cross*). I would try to sing children's tunes occasionally, but Corey only loved the two. I found it a bit odd that those hymns gave a toddler the most comfort and lulled him to sleep.

However, in time, I found it wasn't odd at all. Don't we all find comfort and rest when we cling to the old cross?

As I gazed at my disorganized office, I noticed the cattywampus frames held pictures of the babies who were born and placed in my arms. I recognized the abundant array of papers attached with clips were columns I had written, and I remembered the joy I received from writing them. Under the files on the floor is a book I authored, which I dedicated to God, and a bill I need to pay with money I have in my bank. Ribbons are scattered because a grandchild celebrated a birthday, and the pencils are required to rearrange an overbooked calendar.

It was by God's amazing grace that this disarray belonged to me. If I had no photos to be leveled, or no words to write, or no money to pay the bills, or no events to scribble on a calendar, the office would be clean, but my world would be empty. By God's "mace" grace, my life is full of blessings, even though sometimes I am just too blind to see.

The Old cross I cling to provides the forgiving of my many awful sins and enables me to stumble forward in faith. When my eyes cannot locate the cross, I usually wind up with just a mess. I become overwhelmed, commit more egregious transgressions, and generally fall apart.

I have no idea how folks manage life without faith. The chaos and minutia of life must drive them batty. I get a bit crazy when I cannot locate my iPad, or my keys, or my glasses, but I return to saneness because I have found what is important.

It is simply a cross, which I will cling to until the day when the clutter is all cleaned up, and I view a crown.

God's blessings to you all.

He Speaks to Me Everywhere

AS A CHILD, I learned an old hymn: *This is My Father's World*. I remember being very proud of myself when I could sing a few verses of this hymn and also of *Jesus Loves Me*. Around the same time, I also memorized the prayer, *Now I Lay Me Down to Sleep*. All three have served me very well in my life.

I was born with asthma, and at the time, my parents weren't aware of any medication for this ailment. Many evenings during my childhood, I stayed awake, trying to breathe. The Vicks Vapor Rub and the whine of the vaporizer near my face did little to calm my fear that if I fell asleep, I would not wake up.

On those dark nights when breathing was near impossible, I would rock back and forth on all fours repeating monotonously, "Now I lay me down to sleep. I pray the Lord my soul to keep. If I should die before I wake, I pray the Lord my soul to take."

I discovered the rhythm of the prayer with the rocking would regulate my breathing and, I found a peace that if I did not survive the night, I would awaken in God's arms.

I was seventeen when I finally outgrew asthma, but I never forgot the little prayer, which I believe saved me more nights than I can fathom.

Most all of us know *Jesus Loves Me*. It is probably one of the first songs a preschooler is taught. I can't sing a note, but when I was little, I sure thought I could and would belt this song loudly and proudly while causing discomfort to all the others Jesus loved.

How many times in my life have I thought I was alone and unloved? Those days when my battles with depression took my soul into depths of despair and questioning why I should continue on. Those troubling moments when I felt as if I failed, and hope seemed unattainable.

Yet, somewhere, in the recesses of my heart and mind, I could hear the little girl joyously belting, "Yes, Jesus Loves Me!"

My friend attended a preschool Christmas program to hear her little granddaughter sing. Afterward, I asked her how *Miss Precious* did.

"Well, she belted the song out of tune, oblivious to the fact that she is probably not a small version of Taylor Swift! However, she sang with complete abandon and joy."

Isn't that really all that matters?

The last verse of *This Is My Father's World* rings in my ears today.

This is my Father's world.
He shines in all that's fair
In the rustling grass, I hear him pass
He speaks to me everywhere.

When I reflect over the last six years and realize just how different my life is from what it was, I often ask myself, how did that happen?

I retired from a career, wrote a story that transitioned into weekly columns, which turned into books. I met fabulous folks. And, trust me, I write not for the money because it is very little, but for the words ringing in my ears and for hearing the rustling in the grass. And I wonder why.

Memories flood my mind with things I had long forgotten, and I see folks I once knew long ago as clearly as if they were here today, and I wonder why.

When I see injustice, intolerance, and lack of respect, I get angry enough to write about how God is not tolerant of any of it, and I wonder why I have no fear to do so.

It is because I live in God's world and among His people. I write because I still can't sing a note, but I am still the girl who joyously, thankfully, belts out words because I believe.

I am no saint. I am not a zealot or a preacher, and ask my friends: I am a terrible listener. However, I do hear the whispers of the Lord who gave me a prayer to ease my fear, a song to tell me I am loved, and a Father whose world sends me stories to write.

Meet God's Soldier with a Mission

WHEN I MOVED to LaGrange, Georgia, from Tennessee as a fifteen-year-old, my first Georgia beau was Dan Larry Payne. I possess an old photo showing Dan, sporting a profoundly serious expression, standing beside me. I was wearing a wrist corsage, a pretty yellow dance dress, and a smile across my face.

Our teen romance lasted about two weeks, which was typical for that age, but we remained loyal friends. He married one of my dearest pals, Jo, soon after high school, with the rest of our classmates questioning, "Wonder how long that will last?"

Mr. and Mrs. Payne were members of our wedding party a bit later. And while their marriage still is intact, mine ended years ago. So, our question is answered, "It lasted forever."

Dan's rich heritage included generations of Payne's serving America during the Revolutionary War to the one that was raging in Viet Nam. Dan kept the family history alive by joining the Army Infantry in 1969 after graduating from college. He attended Officers

Candidate School, completed his military obligation, and returned home to work in the private sector. Of course, he thought his service was concluded; however, God intervened and whispered, "No, Dan, it is not."

When Dan accepted the Lord into his life, I doubt he had any idea where that new friendship would lead him. I have learned that whatever God tells you to do, you might as well just go with the flow because there is a purpose for the direction you are to follow.

"Jo, I am being called to preach!" Dan said.

His wife, being the sweet, Christian person she is, responded, "Ok, if that is what the Lord is saying, then I am with you."

After Dan earned a Master of Divinity degree in Baptist Seminary, the young ordained minister with a growing family was spiritually motivated again. "Jo, I would like to rejoin the Army!" This time, neither Jo nor Dan realized his service was only beginning.

Just before he reached the age that would not permit him to reenlist, he worked his way back into the military and to active duty. The former OCS Tactical Officer was now a Chaplain in the United States Army, where he remained in service to our nation for twenty-six years.

By the time 2005 rolled around, Chaplain Dan Payne's country had placed him from Ft. Fort Benning, Georgia, into nine more military bases across our land. He crossed oceans to help his fellow comrades in various Korean assignments, then went to Kuwait as the Command Chaplain for Camp Doha. For his faithful service in aiding so many during Desert Storm/Shield, he was presented the Bronze Star personally by Major General Barry McCaffrey.

Once his military career ended, he had accumulated more medals than I can list in this story, including the Legion of Merit. However, it was not the shiny awards that told of his bravery; it was his courage to follow the path God laid before him, no matter what.

When he was recently nominated and accepted into the US Army Officers Candidate School Hall of Fame, the accolades read, in part, "a fabulous listener, a gifted speaker, a compassionate soul, admired, loved, dedicated, blessed with God-given talent, plus, ready and willing to serve others."

After retiring from military duty, he worked with the US National Park Service, where he served to maintain and protect our parks' beauty from Alaska to Georgia. Jo and Dan continue volunteering to aid veterans, youth, and those needing any assistance throughout America.

Chaplain Dan Larry Payne, the boy with the serious face, grew to be an exemplary leader among men and a humble missionary for God. Perhaps, greatness is found in the one who most unselfishly serves. He is the epitome of the American soldier and citizen.

Dan's patriotism cannot be told by mere words but by those soldiers who share their stories of this unsung American hero. His words, devotion, love for Jo, and fellow men from all walks of life are reminders of what a lifetime of honor is. It is not in the fuss we make or the screams we shout, but instead in the quiet listening of God's direction and the joy one finds in following it.

Our nation is a bit topsy-turvy today. However, like Chaplain Dan, our American narrative lies in those who serve both God and country with integrity, selflessness, and heart.

The Chaplain is battling cancer, and his future is uncertain. Rest assured, however, his earthly glory is no match for what awaits him when he meets his Commander in heaven.

I salute you, my friend; you bless our country with your dedication and wear the armor of God valiantly.

The Mystery Church in the Valley

OCCASIONALLY, I FIND myself believing I can do anything regardless of ability or talent. So, in other words, I probably think too highly of myself. My brain is sometimes fooled by lofty dreams.

Every few years, my mind wants to believe I am an artist. My friend, Gerri, is an artist, and so was Van Gogh. When I view authentic art, my eyes remind me I should just stick to painting by numbers with crayons. But because I am stubborn, recently, I again pulled out the old paintbrushes and pretended to be someone other than who I am.

My friend Deborah and I love old country churches. When I travel to where I was born in Tennessee, there is an overlook off the side of a curvy mountain road, which always beckons to me, urging me to stop. No matter how many times I view the bucolic scene below, joy fills my soul.

A white church is nestled among hardwood trees and farmland. Its distinctive spire, topped with a cross, climbs toward heaven. As my eyes scan the valley, I can almost hear the old hymn *Peace in the Valley* echo in the hills, calming weary souls. I have viewed this vista in all seasons, and even when the green hills turn to gray, it is still beautiful.

For some unknown reason, I decided to try my hand at painting old churches. I found a Christmas card showcasing a country church, which I attempted to replicate on little wooden plaques I planned to give a few friends. They were purposely small, so my pals could hide them when their guests arrived and put them away after the holidays.

Soon, Deborah believed she too could paint churches.

"Come on over, and we can do this together!" I happily told her. "Look on the internet to find a church you like and copy it."

She walked through my back door with a printed copy of the church she wished to paint. It looked familiar with its aged siding, arched windows, and bell tower below a simple cross. By the end of the day, Deborah's brain healed itself of foolish dreams, and she declared, "I am no painter! What was I thinking?" With a wave of her hand, the unfinished attempt at painting the old church was left to me because I still possessed silly illusions of artistic grandeur. I was not yet healed of such madness.

The next day I examined her unfinished church and oddly decided to turn it into a Christmas scene. I added snow, wreaths, and red bows on the adjoining fences. The print showed a lamb standing in front of the church, and when I attempted to paint him, he was perfect. However, I was sane enough to still acknowledge I was living in some self-imposed sugar plum land. Lucky Deborah had escaped.

Once it was finished, I returned the Christmas painting to Deborah and wished her a Merry Christmas. She loved it, and so did my husband, but the scene haunted me. Why did I turn it into a Christmas art, and why did the lamb seem perfect and easy to paint?

A few days later, Deborah and I were doing a bit of shopping. "Oh, my goodness, Lynn, come here!" As I approached her, she held up a box of Christmas cards. It was the same scene I drew with snow and wreaths and bows on fences. There were two lambs instead of one, and the caption was "A Christmas Prayer."

A few days later, I began to decorate my tree. All the ornaments were wrapped in tissue paper to protect them year after year. I picked up a large round one, and when I did, its price tag fell out of the tissue. I must have bought it at the end of the season the previous year and packed it away. When I carefully removed the paper to see what it was, chills crept up my spine. The ornament depicted the church Deborah had copied, the one I finished as a Christmas scene and was now on Christmas cards. I have no idea where I bought it or why.

However, I know that this mystery church reminds me of the church I love in a Tennessee valley. It is not a dream that the lamb is perfect because He is. The scene turned to Christmas because the lamb came to us, offering peace.

And an old hymn continues to echo its way into my heart and hopefully into yours.

There will be peace in the valley for me, someday.
There will be peace in the valley for me, oh Lord, I pray.
There'll be no sadness, no sorrow, no trouble, trouble I see.
There will be peace in the valley for me.

Under the Blue Colorado Sky

HOME FOR MY adult son is the mile-high city of Denver. It is where a cloudless, azure sky envelops the snowcapped Rockies, which sparkle in bright sunlight. Every visit, I am never sure if it is the altitude or the beauty which takes my breath away.

During one long Easter weekend, we traveled to Boulder, home to the University of Colorado. We strolled the brick mall streets downtown where tulips and manicured perfection replaced cars. Street performers filled the air with vibrations from guitars, fiddles, and folk songs.

It was a lively scene dominated by young folks sporting a bit of a hippie vibe. Boulder had changed little from the university town it was in the late 1960s, although it had better restaurants and shops. And instead of barefooted, long-haired '60s hippies, the people I saw on that visit wore sneakers and hair in all colors. Groovy!

The hippies I once knew spread flowers and peace. Some protested, experimented with drugs, and listened to rock music splashed with defiance. Our parents' generation was labeled *the establishment*, and they often believed the world would eventually be doomed by these errant Baby Boomers.

"Their music is horrific; they are all druggies and are not true Americans!" The establishment shouted as the chants of the hippies rose to drown out adverse reactions to their culture.

Most generations believe the next generation will never be as accomplished as they are, and they declare America is going down the tubes. They believe the country is destined to fail because of the bad behavior of irresponsible, crazy kids.

Anybody remember our parents not allowing the boys to wear long hair? Anyone recall the moms and dads condemning the gyrations of Elvis or the mania the Beatles produced?

Well, I wore bell bottoms, owned Elvis albums, and who among Baby Boomer readers didn't watch the Beatles on Ed Sullivan?

But our parents were wrong. We grew up and became productive citizens. The long-haired hippie boy of the '60s is now CEO of some company somewhere, and the flower-child girl at Woodstock is now a grandmother, retired from the company she founded in the '70s.

On Easter Sunday, we attended services near my son's home in Denver. Highlands United Methodist is a noble church, which has seen multiple generations pass through its doors since 1926. The air was crisp, the sky again brightly blue, and, frankly, the scene reminded me of a time forty years earlier when my little boy wore a seersucker suit and carried his Easter basket to church.

Since church attendance had been declining and younger folks had not been participating as much in services across our land, and since I was no longer in the Bible Belt, I wondered what I would see that Easter.

We took our seats in old wooden pews, where I noticed children's storybooks mixed between the Bibles and Methodist hymnals. I thought it was a bit odd, but after a few moments, I understood.

Many children, escorted by parents, noisily ran toward their seats. Toddlers were dressed in Easter colors of blue, pink, yellow, and purple. Siblings with disheveled hair and infants cradled in their parents' arms filled every seat in the old church.

Finally, the sanctuary was alive with songs, babies crying, children jabbering, and happiness. The 1960s hippie had become the grandparent. He sat beside the 1980s college student who had become the parent who sat beside the child who was reading the book he'd pulled from the back of the pew.

The young minister, wearing a peach-colored Easter blazer, enthusiastically stood to welcome all. After old Easter hymns were sung, he delivered a rip-roaring, happy sermon filled with God's word and celebration for the risen Lord.

The world isn't doomed because young folks listen to rap music instead of the Beatles or Guns N' Roses. America isn't lost because a newbie hippie is dressed in ragged khakis with purple hair and rings in his nose.

I found hope and solace in witnessing the return of young families to worship the Lord. One generation will pass on the word of God to the next. As I studied the congregation, I was pretty sure the grandmother in front of me once wore a flower in her hair, and the toddler's father once followed the Grateful Dead.

No, the world isn't doomed if we continue to pass our faith forward so the five-year-old boy in the seersucker suit may one day return to find hope in a church under a blue Colorado sky.

Surviving Our Worst Thanksgiving Day

HAVE YOU EVER noticed that most of us remember our worst Thanksgivings? The time the turkey burned, or the time when we were so ill on Turkey Day, we could only stomach a cracker? The truth is some folks will experience their first, worst Thanksgiving this year. No matter the year. The year that I write this. The year that you read it. Somewhere, someone will have a tough time of it. However, I pray they keep heart because there is a secret hidden amid difficulty or pain.

Years ago, just before a Thanksgiving Day in the early 1980s, I was admitted to the hospital for extreme exhaustion. I didn't burn the turkey, rather I was the one that was burned—mentally and physically burned out. It was a terrible time when distress and sadness enveloped me. If I attempted any chore, my heart would race, and my head would pound as if my thirty-something-year-old body were giving up or tuning out.

At the time, I was newly divorced with three small children who were looking forward to Thanksgiving Day. The dog had given birth to puppies, the turkey was thawing in the fridge, and my recipes were scattered among work papers and laundry. Yet here it was the Wednesday night before Thanksgiving Thursday, and I was staring at the ceiling of a hospital room.

Thankfully, my children were safely in their father's care and traveling to their grandparents' home miles away to celebrate the day. My mother and father were planning to drive north from their home in Florida after Thanksgiving to help. No other family members lived in Georgia, and for the first time, I faced Thanksgiving alone.

Tears began to stream down my face turning into downpours. A nurse came into my room and sat on the edge of my bed. She said little but took my hand and held it tightly until the tears dried, and I fell into a deep sleep.

When morning ushered in the dreaded Thanksgiving, I prayed that God would somehow speed up the day for those of us who were in the hospital, and it would be over. However, every minute seemed like an hour, and the only thing that was speeding was my racing heart.

When it was time for lunch, the nurse came into my room with a wheelchair. "Hop in, girl, we are going to have Thanksgiving dinner!" she cheerfully commanded.

"I don't feel like it." I quietly responded.

She was a somewhat intimidating nurse with a stern demeanor, and when she said, "You don't have a choice!" I knew I didn't. With a scowl on my face and tears beginning to pool, she took me into a room where several round tables were covered in white tablecloths.

Each table was decorated with turkeys, formed from construction paper in various colors, and a tiny vase holding one flower. Most of the patients had families who joined them with small children in tow. Around my table, with its purple-paper-turkey centerpiece, sat those of us who were without family, plus the nurse.

I took a deep breath and prayed for aid to survive my utter isolation and overwhelming gloom. When we thanked God for our blessings, I didn't feel very blessed at all. And by the look on their faces, neither did anyone else who was sitting with me.

As I tried to eat the cafeteria turkey and dressing, I studied the folks who were beside me. We were an assembly of strangers with individual stories and various illnesses. We were of all ages, of various ethnicities, and living different lives. Yet, we were holding hands and thanking God for all we had.

Out of the blue—and to this day, I have no idea why—I remember suddenly sensing it was my responsibility to spread cheer to this abandoned-looking group. To my utter surprise, by the time the tasteless pecan pie was served, our wheelchairs were shaking with laughter.

After two weeks, I returned home, life resumed, and Thanksgivings were never the same again. Every year when that special Thursday rolls around in November, and as I decorate my table with candles and a cornucopia, I always recall the purple paper turkey on the hospital dining table. Each time I offer a Thanksgiving prayer, I thank God for the laughter He gifted me on my saddest holiday. When I view my family gathered around our Thanksgiving table, I recall the strangers who once held my hands to pray. It was the *faith* we all embraced that stressful day that eased our pain and turned strangers into friends.

This Thanksgiving, and every Thanksgiving, when remembering our blessings, let us also offer a passionate prayer for those suffering from illness, homelessness, or grief.

My worst Thanksgiving made me more appreciative for all the holidays that would follow, and I am incredibly thankful for the God who holds my hand through them all.

Relinquishing My Christmas Crown

EVERY YEAR, ON December 26th, I contemplate abdicating my throne as the Queen of Christmas. I ponder such a thought each year after Santa visits because I am usually bone-tired, but in 2020 it was different. Perhaps, it was not fatigue from cooking or cleaning, but rather a tiredness from a year when all things seemed exhausting and good news was in short supply.

My lack of positive energy could have been due, in part, to my two-year-old refrigerator. It had broken three days before Christmas and would be on the fritz until January. Thank goodness we had the old workhorse fridge in the garage. But, what a pain!

The same day the refrigerator broke, friends came to sing Christmas carols in the evening. When the doorbell rang, my daughter's dog started to bark and headed for the door. When the big friendly pup tried to escape, I held him by his collar. Once he saw those smiling faces and heard the word, "Hark," he bolted just enough to throw me off my small porch stoop and into the bushes where my head ran into a brick wall.

The cracking sound of my head hitting bricks was so loud, the carolers heard it and assumed I was a goner. But alas, on the day after Christmas I was still living. Yes, I was battered and bruised in places I forgot existed, but to my amazement, I was back to picking up dog toys, cookie crumbs, and glitter after a day of rest. I guess Mama was right about me being hard-headed after all!

So, Christmas came and went, and I was ready to quickly pack it away for the first time in my life. Because I was the Queen of Christmas, I typically waited until the neighbors began to complain about the reindeer still on the porch around Easter. However, that year, putting away Christmas early seemed the right thing to do. I started boxing my many decorations.

The holiday season was not the same for most of us that year. As much as I'd tried to focus on the glory found in Christ's birth, the day was unusual and challenging. People everywhere were worried about income, food, and a killing virus. We lived day to day, hoping that we would survive financially, and our loved ones would stay healthy. Most every day of 2020 had tested our strength and faith. It was difficult to comprehend how many had lost so much in one year.

On top of a pandemic, we had been bombarded with misinformation, scare tactics, and competing theories. In my opinion, the far right and far left needed to take sharp turns and travel toward the middle of the road. Neither of the far sides was leading us on the path to healing. Mostly they were inciting anger and fueling distrust, which was extraordinarily sad.

Soon after the holidays, I was alone in my bedroom listening to Alexa playing *Ava Maria*, and I knew it was time to talk to the Lord.

"God, I believe I am going to stop wearing my *Queen of Christmas* crown. The world has gone to the dogs, and the dogs are driving me into brick walls. A bit of my faith in myself and humanity seems lost because of the viciousness of the vying political parties and hateful, angry people. Folks are hungry, yet I pitched a royal fit over my food-filled refrigerator that is on the fritz.

"Many of my family members live in Nashville where a bomb caused horror as bricks from downtown buildings fell over their streets. Fear gripped their Christmas day while I worried about my brick-cracked head. How silly and how selfish I am. Forgive me, Lord."

And then a peace fell over me. As I packed away the fancy ornaments and labeled the boxes for 2021, I realized there was much to throw away from the year 2020. However, I needed to be careful not to box up love, kindness, and compassion. The world would need those to clearly hear, with joy and elation, *Hark, the Herald Angels Sing* when Christmas returned in 2021.

Hate, anger, bullying, and distrust will drive our heads into brick walls, and we could so easily lose faith. And that we simply must not do. If we do, then what would be the point of Christmas? I felt the Lord was calling us to stand in the light of the angels, to heed the call to believe, and to forge onward with dignity, courage, and hope.

So, I put away the grief 2020 caused and polished my old crown. I laid it in the lap of the newborn king where it belonged and where good news and peace always gloriously reign.

Acknowledgements

THERE ARE MANY to thank for all they do to make my life complete. I appreciate you and love you all.

To the readers of my columns, there are endless hugs. For those who send me notes encouraging me to continue writing, you are the icing on the cake and the ribbons on the gift.

David Plazas, Alex Hubbard, Donna Cruze, and Maria De Varenne are the sweet souls who often publish my words in their USA Today network, and I thank you all. How grateful I am for your professionalism, generosity, and expertise.

To lovely Diane Wagner, J.K. Murphy, and all the Times-Journal news staff in Georgia, you are so appreciated by this old gal whom you allow to grace your pages once a week.

For Daniel Evans, Boone Newspapers, and their former editor, Matthew Strother, there are not enough words. I will forever be grateful to you for allowing me to share my heart with your readers. It was you who took a chance, gave me a shot, and published my first sentence. But, no, there are not enough words.

To Allison St. Claire, founder of Senior Wire, what can I say? You are a gift to all the writers who are blessed to know you. Your humor, advice, and hard work inspire us all.

To Carol Fitzgerald, founder and president of The Book Reporter Network, who creates, encourages, and cares not only for best-selling authors, but sends little me *hugs* and never fails to amaze me that she does.

Michaele Flynn Prince, you are the most admirable, most talented artist who makes my pages come alive not only with your pens but with your heart. I love you.

Thank you, Sally Apokedak, for your skill and talent to bind my stories together and create *Southern Comfort*. Your expertise amazes me!

Sir Lee Walburn, talk about icing on the cake! Whoa! What a blessing you are to me. I fall on your every word and am honored to know the 'Knight of Writing.' Lewis Grizzard, Terry Kay, and Celestine Sibley are all applauding their friendship with you from Heaven. How grateful I am to join their adoration. I will forever be your humble friend, Lady Lynn.

Jake Behr, you indeed are one of those angels God sent to cross my path. How blessed am I?

How much do I love my LaGrange High classmates for your unwavering support and friendship through all these years? There is no heart big enough to return the love. You still accept my Tennessee accent, my running mouth, and crazy ways. God bless you all!

Deborah Carter Kerr, you are my soul sister. I am now, and always will be, in awe of you. God truly blessed me when he moved me next door to an angel. And to my other sister, Patricia Walker, I cannot thank you enough for always believing I could do more than most folks thought.

To Richie Mahaffey, my soul brother, I will love you even when we live on the same street in Heaven.

John Wade Freeman, Rich Crofton, Steve Lynn, and Whit Fackler understand who Mama Lynn is, and she adores you all.

Dan and Jo Payne, what an inspiration to all of us! I am honored and humbled to write your story and be your friend.

To Sunshine Shirley Carter, my pal, who sends me a photo of my column every Tuesday Morning when it appears in the MDJ, I thank you. My Tuesdays always start with a smile and your warm heart.

Michele Thomas, Ricki Vann, Bonnie Rademacher, Kitty Keeling, and Geri Harkins, thank you for bringing this book to life with your stories, advice, and ability to put up with me. I treasure you all.

I am not sure how to acknowledge a town, but Monterey, Tennessee, I thank you. You welcomed me back to my ancestral home with open arms. There would be few stories if you were not a part of who I am. I am related to most of those who live in this mountain town and proud to say that I am.

For all the Vietnam Veterans and their families, thank you for so graciously accepting me into your honorable fold. You are my heroes. More importantly, thank you for your service, sacrifice, and courage.

To my niece, Emily Schneller, and nephew, David Walker, and their families, I couldn't cherish you more and am delighted to be your Crazy Aunt Lynn!

For cousin Bob Walker, thank you for being you and reminding me how thankful and honored I am to carry our name and for the folks it represents. So glad the lost cousins are found.

To my family: David Gendusa; Amy Lockman; Heather Nystrum and daughter, Avery; Corey Lockman and Kendra Curtis; Kimberly Gendusa and son, Jax Fender; Kristin and Michael Mascari along with their children, Carter, and Weston; I will always understand you are a gift loaned to me by God. I am so proud of you all and hope that whatever legacy I leave will be one that makes you smile.

Grandpa, Grandaddy, Granny Rose, Lou Ray Walker, Mollie Sparks, Mama, Daddy, Aunt Mary Ruth, my brother, John, and all my family in Heaven, I kept your stories and lessons in my heart, and I shared them. I hope, in some way, I made you proud.

Finally, to God, my friend, Father, and the author of my soul, I love you with all my heart and thank you for the gifts of these people and all the blessings they and you have given me. Thank you for letting me be your typist and reminding me of the commitment I made to you long ago …

"God, I promise, one day I will write a story."

About the Author

AFTER FORTY-THREE YEARS as an Interior Designer in Atlanta, Georgia, Lynn Walker Gendusa put away the tape measure and picked up a pen.

She began writing weekly columns for her adopted hometown newspaper, *The LaGrange Daily News*, in 2015. Her words about home, life, faith, family, and struggles quickly spread.

Lynn became a weekly columnist for the *Times Journal News* in Georgia, which includes *Rome News-Tribune, Marietta Daily Journal,* and other Georgia publications. She also is a weekly columnist for the *Neighborhood News* and her work appears in different venues across America, as well as on MSN.com.

She is regularly featured in the USA Today Networks around the country, including their *Tennessean,* which is especially close to her heart. In addition, her stories appear in senior magazines across the US as well as in *Guideposts.*

Her first book, *It's All WRITE with Me! Essays from my heart,* was published in 2018, and was well received.

She continues to write weekly columns to inspire folks to never give up and never give in—to unite, love, and appreciate each other and God.

Lynn currently resides in Roswell, Georgia, with her husband, David. She is the mother to three grown children, two stepchildren, and grandmother to four.

You can reach Lynn at lynngendusa.com, where you will also find her weekly columns on her blog.

Made in the USA
Columbia, SC
26 September 2021